Beyond The Veil Press

I0476073

TEA WITH MY MONSTER

Poetry & Art
Mental Health Awareness Anthology
Summer 2022

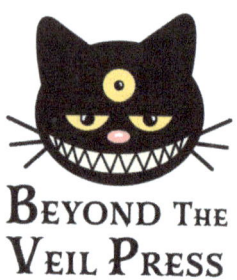

BEYOND THE VEIL PRESS

Anthology © 2022 Beyond The Veil Press

Title © Sophia Mihailidis
Cover Photo © Melia Donk

Printed in the United States of America.

ISBN: 978-1-4357-7107-9

CONTENTS

Note to the Reader

Dear Reader,

An artist gives of themself with every letter, every brushstroke, and every performance. Creating is a true act of vulnerability, a willingness to explore the depths of ourselves and our environments, and to offer that account – in all its splendid fractures – to others.

Likewise, to engage with art is to become part of the story, to enter a narrative beyond our control and to brave connection, conflict, and questioning.

This anthology is an extension of our first, *There Is a Monster Inside That I Am Learning to Love.* This collection tells of challenge, survival, and reclamation. There is struggle, and there is hope. We are so grateful to each contributor for their offering – for an invitation to *Tea With My Monster.* It is an intimate gathering and we're glad you're here.

Special thanks to **Sophia Mihailidis** for gifting us the title and **Melia Donk** for inspiring the cover art.

Warmly,
AJ Wojtalik (she/her)
Beyond The Veil Press

Trigger Warning

Some of the poems in this book may contain mentions of rape, incest, depression, self-harm, and/or suicide.

Please take care of yourself as you read through these experiences and reach out for help if you need it. You are not alone.

US — *Suicide Prevention Line: 1.800.273.8255*
Sexual Assault Hotline: 1.800.656.4673
Domestic Violence Hotline: 1.800.799.7233
Substance Abuse Hotline: 1.800.662.4357
Self-Harm Textline: Text "Connect" to 741741

UK — *Samaritans 116 123*

Australia — Lifeline Australia 13 11 14
Beyond Blue 1300 22 4636

More resources at the back of this book and on our website.

Tea With My Monster

RADIO VOLUME HERO
ag (@written_by_ag)

my body is held hostage by my mind,
the ransom - my time, patience, stability;
my death will come in fours and flickering lights,
twice locked doors to keep out the compulsions,
a prayer to evade the obsession;
my hands move mountains and stop time,
softly, without disturbance,
with careful consideration of the fragility,
no one will die today.

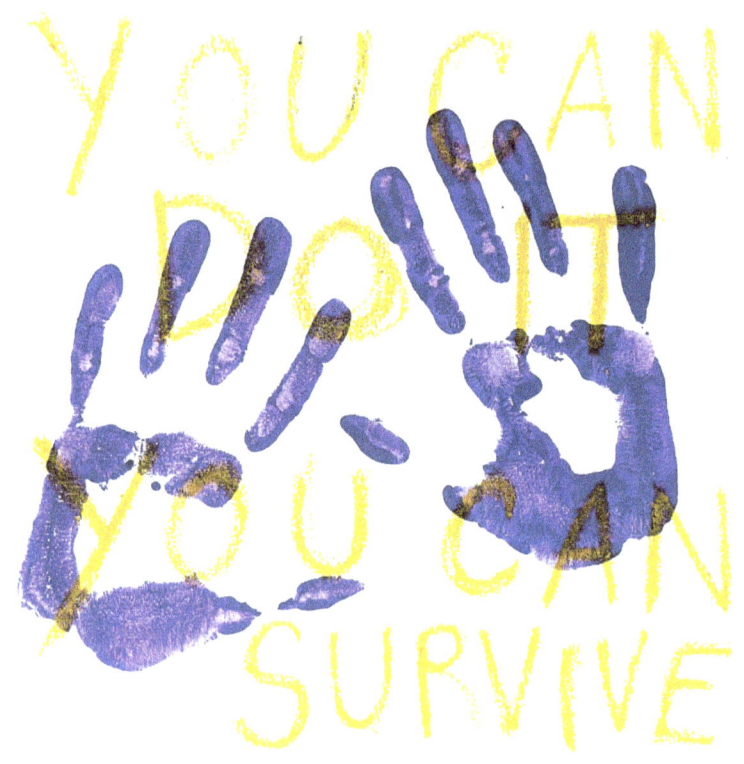

YOU CAN SURVIVE
ag (@written_by_ag)

ACT 3, SCENE 1
ag (@written_by_ag)

the rules of engagement:
i am the same person
made up of all the same things,
particular addition,
all alike,
the execution grapples you,
Love,
sickly,
in death,
perfect,
compelled;
i am one,
incensed to
spite the world,
so weary with chance,
mend,
  perform,
    command.

CLOSURE
AJ Wojtalik (@ajwojtalik.poetry)

most mornings I rage
seething last words
burying your ghost
under taut bedsheets
where you'll wait
I know
and we will dance again
tonight
every night
until I am finished saying
everything you never heard
and I will finally wake up
alone

CAT'S CRADLE
Amanda Roth (@amandarothpoetry)

My fingers wandered
through looped rope
to make diamonds,
ladders, and a leash
for the wild creature
called Hope.

But somewhere between
burnout and babies,
my careful game
of control collapsed,
and Hope slipped away
into the night.

I'm old enough
to know this
is what Hope does,
but also young
enough to be
disappointed.

When she returns
to my porch,
she is feral
and bares her teeth
when she hears me
howling for her.

She stays
long enough
to draw blood
before running
back
into the night.

MY MOTHER GAVE BIRTH TO A DRAGON
Amanda Roth (@amandarothpoetry)

She swallowed an ember,
and I was born,
a blaze in my belly.

I tried to be a child
but when I breathe, walls collapse;
when I cry, it rains flame.

How many nights
did I try to claw
out of reptilian skin?

I breathe fire,
you held out a torch,
and everything changed.

DISUNION OF HEART AND MIND
Amy Zender

it carves the grandest canyon,
miles deep and equally as wide
into my heart, thousands of paper cuts
only to wickedly sting
from the salt of my cascade of tears

nevermind the choking chains
braided around my lungs
stifling breaths of life
sandpaper hugs and sympathetic glances
leave me gutted and wanting

if you phone
don't expect words from the lexophile
to whom you've grown accustomed
for now i only whisper
broken sounds of sadness

i do not sit in a space of unsaids
i walk alone through tenebrous voids
your nourishment is tasteless
your light burns my eyes
your grace paralyzes me

a thin faint line separates heart and mind
that is where the soul resides
playing peacekeeper
weeping for both casualties
my heart wails as the mind misplaces

the beast that licks at my neck
clutches into my spine flesh,
so heavily, i walk on my knees
it enters and exits as it pleases
i am its plaything

before you ask, how are you
my heart has a double barrel shotgun blast
through which i leak love daily
night brings no absolution
days offer no clemency

as my heart grieves what my mind suffers

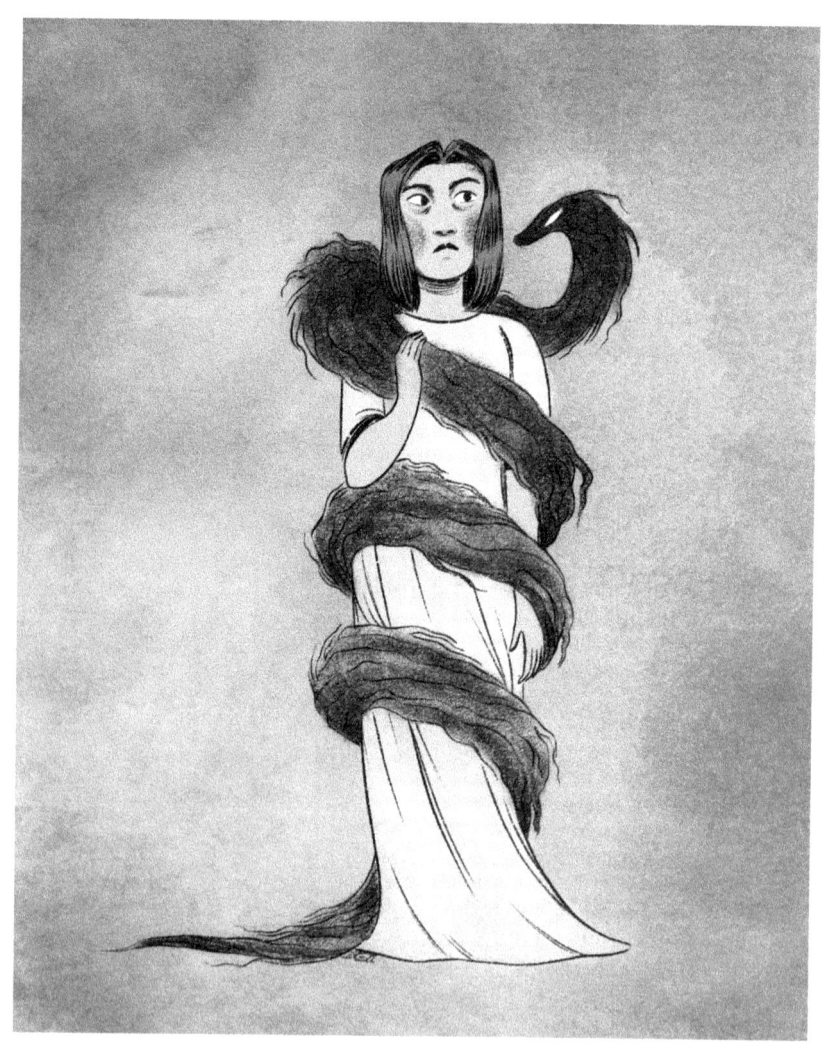

DRAPED
Emily Ericson (@emilyeillustration) Digital.

THIS MIRROR LIKE GOD
Angela Marshall (@angela_writes_life_and_loss)

I stopped believing in God.
In a higher power who somehow had control of my fate.
A mythical being judging me and determining my worth.
I fell out with God. He wasn't there when I needed Him.
A God shouldn't make you suffer to see how strong you are.

I have replaced God.
There is something else which judges me.
Questions me and the sins of my everyday life.
Illustrating my choices back to me, absorbed not reflected.
Turning my thoughts inside of me. Stabbing with tiny swords.

It is not a God but God-like.
My unspoken confession of sins written all over me
in the size of my thighs, my hips and my stomach.
In the rolls of fat that appear
following on from another binge.

I cannot avoid this God.
They appear everywhere, telling their twisted truths.
How I have failed, again and again.
Destined for hell, another twist of fate.
An ugly devil sitting on my shoulder.

I can smash this God.
I won't. It would cut and bleed.
Create questions I couldn't answer.
It shouldn't be a God.
This mirror, judging my every bite.

OCTOBER, 2016
Anne Walsh Donnelly (@annewalshdonnellypoetry)

Jaws of a bench-vice clamp my temples.
My shoulders list under the weight
of a bag of slack.

My mouth belches exhaust fumes.
A concrete mixer masticates sludge
in my stomach. I shuffle

on feet glued to flagstones.
Skin tarred and feathered,
by the depression that steals

dopamine from my hacked brain.
A hammer smashes my breastbone,
exposing my prune heart.

I slither down mucky slopes,
daughter's skipping rope in one hand,
unopened blister pack of pills in the other.

GROWTH

Cait Thomson (@cait.t.poetry)

it's surreal to come across things growing
where they have no business surviving
the grass shooting through a crack in the driveway
the roses climbing a chain link fence in an alley
the pumpkin vine creeping from the compost bin
the onion shoot in a cup of baja blast
no, not just surviving or   growing
but thriving
                blooming
                        e x p l o   d   i   n   g

one day i should like to be so powerful
that my loud desperation to live
could bend the very laws of nature
instead, i am the quiet whimper
of a woman shaken by her own shadow
but i can't help but wonder
if its time to root where i've fallen
and grow

SMALL, FRANTIC
Cait Thompson (@cait.t.poetry)

today i am a mouse
tomorrow, maybe a robin
or perhaps a bumble bee
but for today, definitely mouse

beady eyes darting
fragile chest heaving
every muscle tensed
at the ready
jumping at every
doorbell / pot drop / drawer slam

i have just one real predator
and there is no outrunning it
only embracing it

i am ready to devote
the rest of this life
convincing my body
i am not a small, frantic creature
anymore

A CAT CURLED INSIDE

Caitlan Docherty (@cmnpoetry)

sleep infected with day's sparse, polite grammar.
the truth left in chewed pen caps, lunchtime's
slim, striped straws in cold cans of diet pepsi.
invisible ink arranged a name
: letter by letter, wafer-delicate on blue
college-ruled notebook paper. c's
first crook begot a pure
hollow, unfilled
semicircle with room
for wanting. every late august
breathed brittle—auburn
wake of early-incurving leaves, self-fulfilling
prophecy, bitter crunch. naked, rain
-blackened branches and all fruit labored for, charred.
lopsided mattress, empty bed, smoke sheets, a cat
curled inside the meek interim of acceptable grieving.

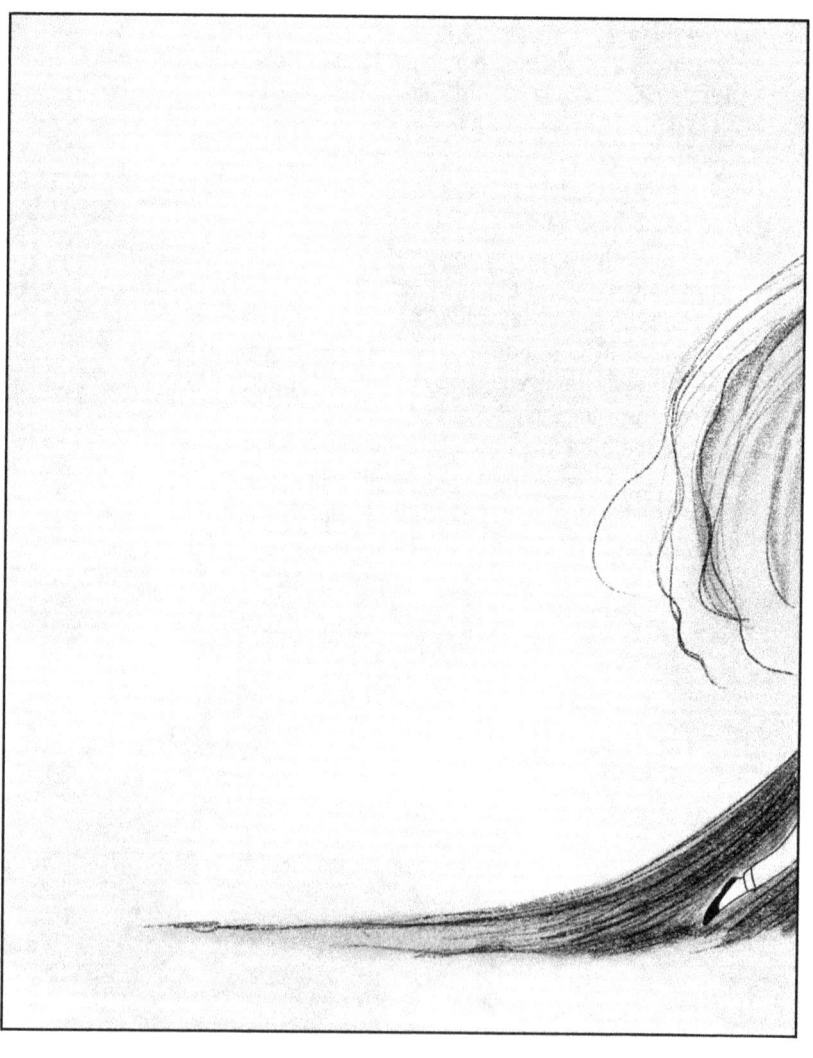

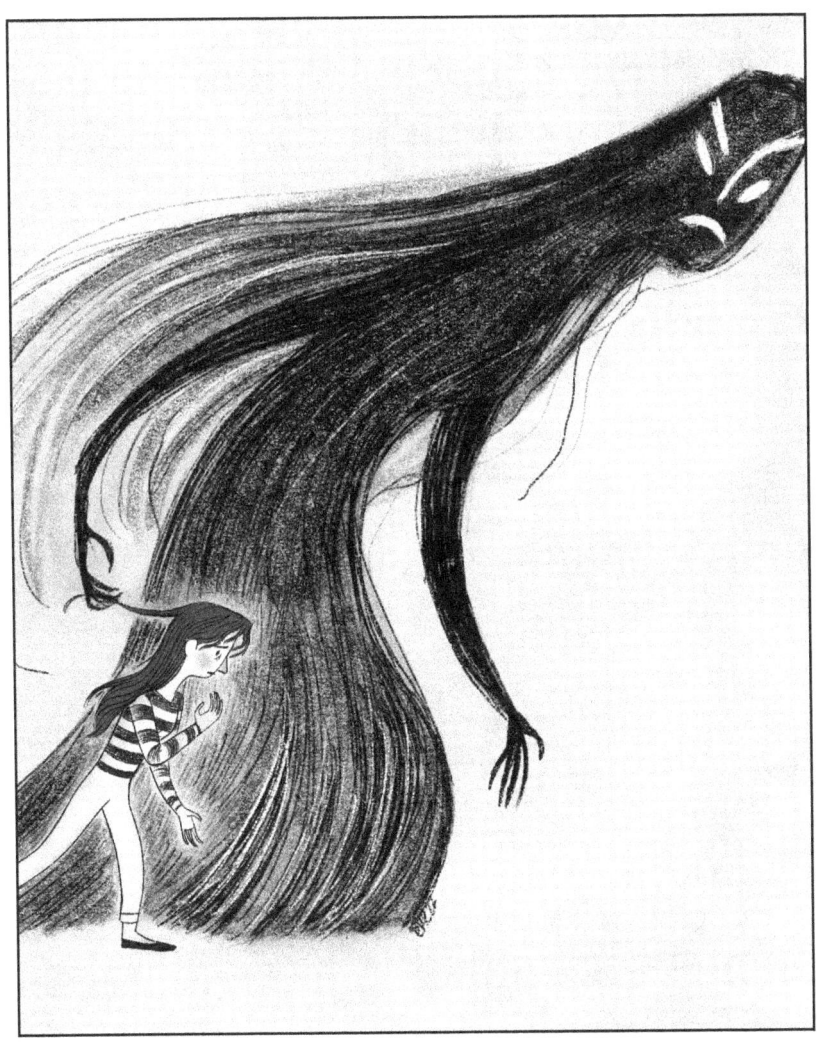

SHADOWED
Emily Ericson (@emilyeillustration) Digital.

STARLIGHT

Catherine Hamilton (@cathamcreates)

Some days I want to escape from all of this
There's too much in this world that can hurt you
Things I can no longer cure with a kiss
Days become things just to get through
I want to run, I know you do too
In a world that contains so much darkness
I must dig into the bones of you
Plant you with starlight and kindness

REJUVINATION
Catherine Hamilton (@cathamcreates)

Rain floods the burn
Crashing over jagged rocks
I want to climb in
Have it scrub me clean

I cried myself a river
Now I'm trying not to drown

Birds flit and dart
They move so quick
So free, so easy
I look on with envy

I cried myself a lake
Now I float in my lament

Thirsty from saline seas
Trapped inside a monster
I am my own hostage
Longing for rejuvenation

I cried myself an ocean
Now I must teach myself to swim

ONE, TWO, THREE
Celine de Moor (@photographs_by_celine)

Horrors in my head,
make me do this.
Horrors in my head,
make me scared.

Horrors in my head,
make me count to three.
Horrors in my head,
make it hard to breathe.

I pick up my hand,
not left,
but right.

one,
        two,
                three.
one,
        two,
                three.

Mum says goodnight.
I have to say it last.
Otherwise,
something will happen to her.
Otherwise,
she will be gone.

I forgot to brush my teeth.

I jump out of bed.
Stepping out of my room,
with my right foot.
Closing the door,
with my right hand.

Brushing for two minutes,
until it buzzes three times.
I have to end at my front teeth at the lower part.
Otherwise,
I will gain weight.
Otherwise,
I will be fat.

I smile in the mirror,
before I turn of the light.
Otherwise,
bad things will happen.
Otherwise,
I will not come back.

Stepping with my right foot,
into my bedroom.

Mum has to come again,
to tell me goodnight.
I give her a big kiss,
and at last I say to her:
sleep tight.

I turn off my lamp,
with my right hand.

one,
      two,
            three
one,
      two,
            three

After this lightshow,
my day has finally come to an end.

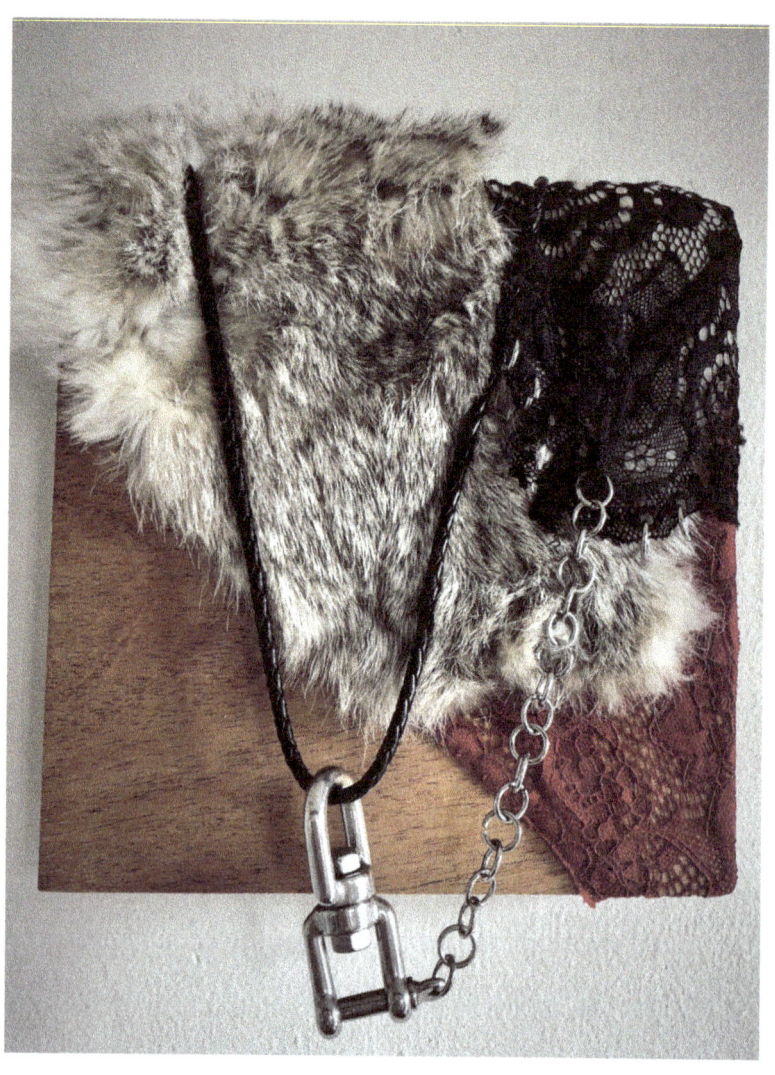

HOLD BACK THE GHOSTS
Emily Perina (@esp_sculpture) 2019.
Fur, lace, wood, steel. 8"x8".

I TRY TO WRITE A POEM WHILE MY BEST FRIEND
GETS A KETAMINE INFUSION FOR HER DEPRESSION
Courtney LeBlanc (@wordperv79)

Like the Mariana Trench, I imagine a hole
darker and deeper than I've ever seen
in real life. It's not filled with spiders
or lizards or cobwebs or spindly roots –
it's just black and endless. This is my best
friend's depression, a hole so fathomless
she told her therapist she can do it
for five more years. *It* being life – living
and breathing and existing. So they're trying
something new, a drug that isn't fully
understood dancing with a brain that isn't
fully understood. She cries a little and says
bits of nonsense as the clear liquid waltzes
down the tube and into her vein. I sit
in the room with her, watching and waiting
for the drug to work its magic, to make
the right connections, to stop the sad
from winning.

THE CASTING
d.h.miller (@d.h.miller_penned)

She has returned to me
My dark lover
She bids me lie with her
Beneath the sheets
Where we can be intertwined
Inextricable from the other

Artful liar, I believe
Her whispered deceit
She soothes me in muted tones
The world fades enfolded in her maw
I will succumb to her as
She spells me unworthy

Oh, loveless bitch
She'll release me to my knees
Vanquished by our embrace
Left only to retreat
Beneath cold sheets
Smothered in her, forgotten

THE BUSY SIDEWALKS OF EDEN
Daniel Reyes (@xanielreyes)

haunted
or chemical imbalance?
quarrels with the afterlife
only the judge can heal
time wasted
no rewinds or backstrokes
scrolling through my demons
what should haunt me today?
God, the scarecrow?
I, the black bird
teleporting flesh
from the pavement
to my belly
every cornfield
or the truth
forbidden fruit

FROZEN CHARLOTTE

David Estringel (@david_estringel)
Originally published by Cajun Mutt Press.

Skin, blue,
like mistletoe berries
under her midnight sun, she
sways and hums
to the tune of fireflies
in flight
and whispers upon the wind
through bare branches.
Night's chill rests, warm,
upon bare shoulders
in want of cover, but
the anima
and blood
are numb to Winter's sting.
So, she dances,
the wreath of Spring,
long fallen away,
beyond the crystalline grasp
of icy fingertips
(or loving hands).
Falling
silent and still—
a night heron frozen, midflight—
she turns, slowly,
to me
and the offending glow
of yellow lamplight
on bedroom walls (reflected in my eyes),
until thoughts pull her
away
in cold procession
back
into the taciturn embrace of
Night's song
and that baleful moon, above.
So,
she dances,
unknowing (uncaring)
that she'll be alone
for the next thaw.

A DREAMCATCHER IN THE RYE
Eddie Brophy (@eddiebrophywriter)

The subterfuge of narcissists
and a lineage of sociopaths
goaded a masochistic rapport
with a fallacy I called family
and now the vagrant specters
of a cumbersome childhood
are looking to find refuge
inside their innocent heads
and interlope on their sublime
arcane truths about happiness
and like a tapeworm of depression
they will imbibe every precious memory
because I have watched this nefarious disease
covet too many futures
until it monopolized an entire generation
I do not want the pools of blue and brown
to be reflections of a loneliness
that was not content enough with killing me
and maybe its neurotic superstition
or the anachronistic exorcists condemning
the desecration of a youthful exuberance
that collapsed upon itself
like a dreamcatcher in the rye
I want their love to be sustained
with the finesse of integrity
only someone who has seen the underbelly can provide

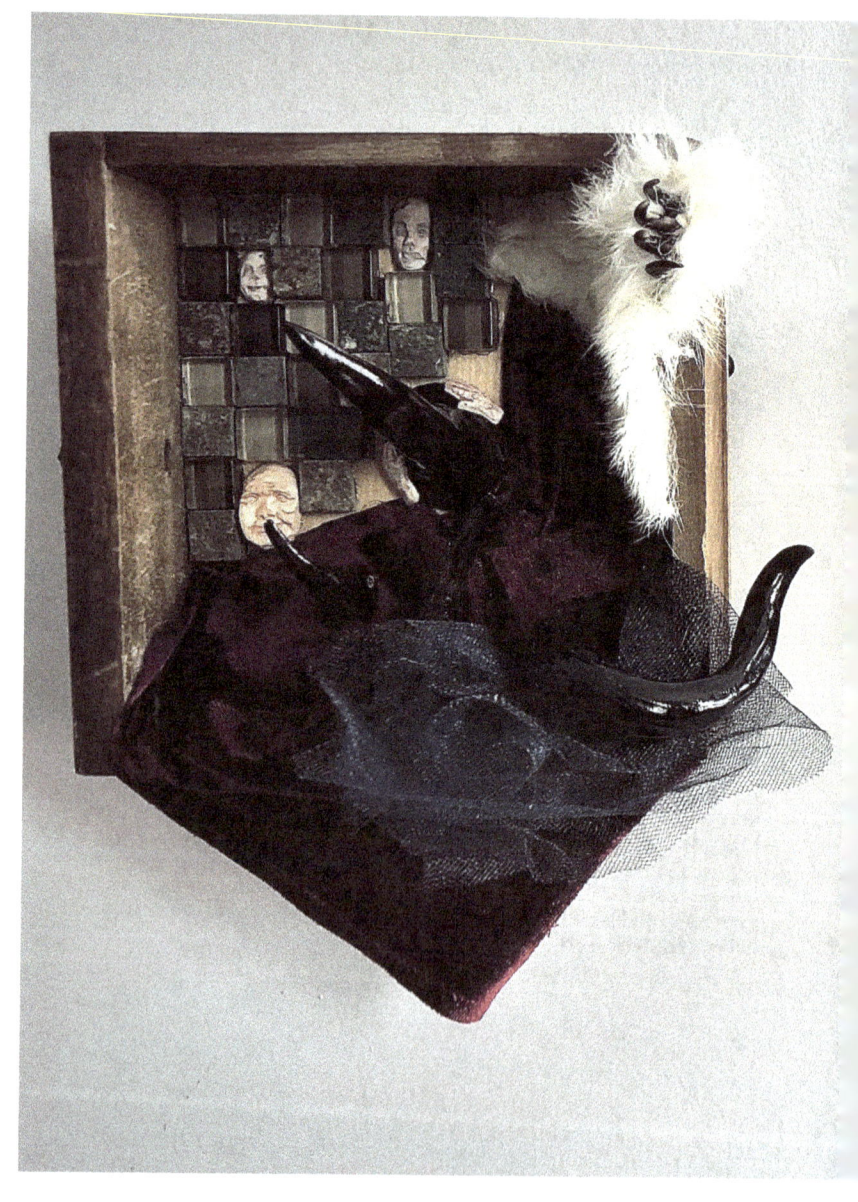

HIS AND HERS
Emily Perina (@esp_sculpture) 2021.
Mixed Media. 7"x8".

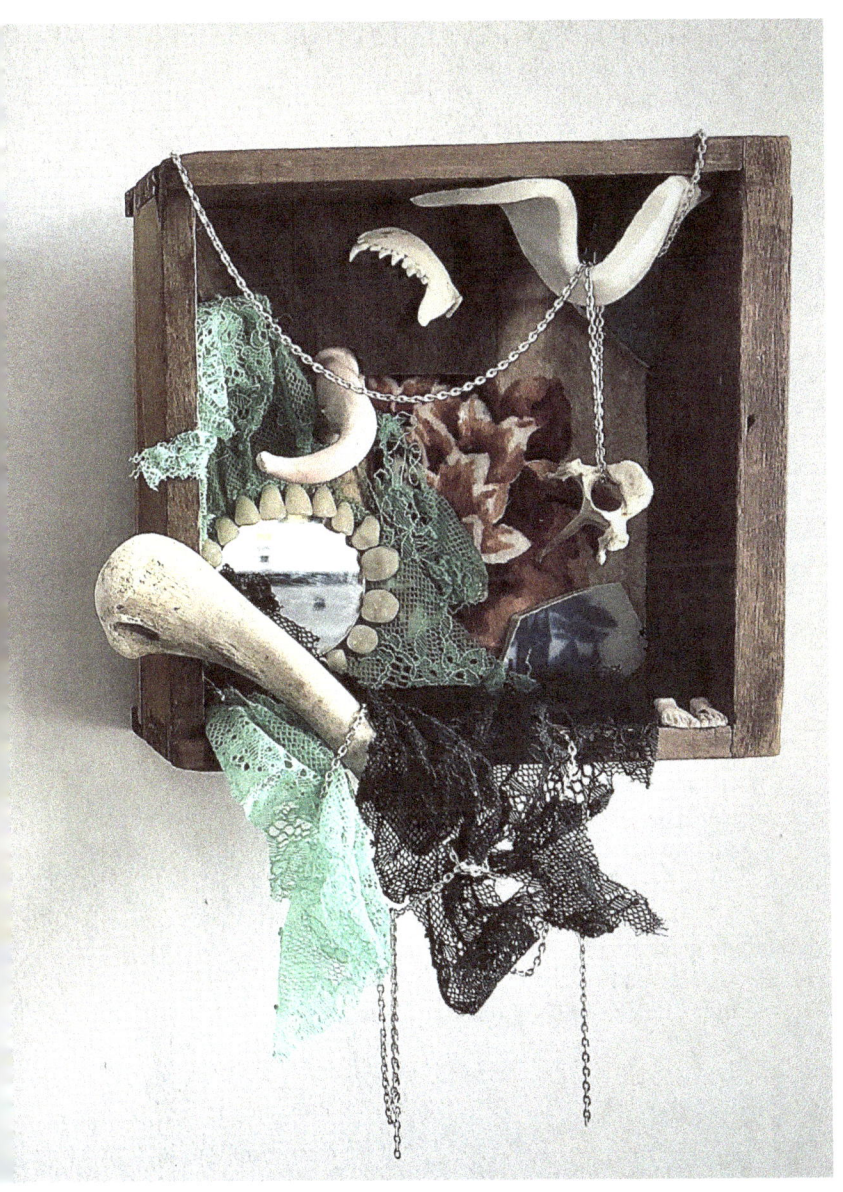

AT LEAST THE WAR IS OVER NOW
Elaine T Stockdale (@e.tstockdale_)
After Camille Sarah

My body is not a temple it's a wishing well,
throw what you have to spare or what's left of you
and I'll see what I can do.

But it's not a shrine, I'm no hero, no saint,
no one kneels daily before me.
So don't expect a miracle – an answer to your prayers.

My body is not a temple, in fact it's a battleground
but I'm the only soldier left in the war,
and I fight myself profusely every day.

My body is a boxing bag.
I beat myself in senseless rage for all my stupid mistakes.
My fists bleed for the mountain of regrets I contain
and it's peak so sharp that it cuts through my brain.
Combined with a KO and I'm out,
ghosts of the past left to nail my body to a cross –
but I'm no saviour, I'm no big loss.

I was the rush hour train you dreaded
but you rode anyway,
only used to get to where you needed to be –
fast.

My body is not a temple. It was a ticking time bomb,
and nobody wanted to make my heart a forever home.
Because they knew eventually one day I'd explode.

ALEXA
Elaine T Stockdale (@e.tstockdale_)

Alexa, can you turn off the voices in my head?
Play my favourite songs instead.
When I'm lying-in bed my thoughts I dread
all my life negativity I've been fed.

Am I better off alive or better off dead?
Rest in peace, out of my head.
Play me something motivational
to change my thinking,
further underground I'm slowly sinking.

Alexa, can you turn on the lights in here?
In the dark of my mind I live in fear.
It's a constant battle when the war is in me
every single day I just want to be free.

Alexa
are you there?

Can you
hear me?

/THE TRIGGER IS IN THE TRAUMA/

Emily Perkovich (@undermeyou)

We're

/healing, we're healing/

but the path to

/healed/

is something like tumbling down the throat of a giant. Chasm of infinity.
Sempiternal-stumble. And we keep saying

/attempted suicide recovery/

but the words come out choked, because if we're honest, that noose is still
neat around our necks. And how can we do anything but stutter the words
when we are so lacking in what it takes to breathe? We keep saying

/trauma-victim survivor/

like after the

/abuser/

walked out the door the

/abuse/

followed suit, but it's made a bed in the dark spots between our bones.
This garden is in need of culling, and we've misplaced the means to tend
these crops. And sometimes the

/suffering/

is in the leaving itself.

/Abandonment/

doesn't end with the closing of the book. The words pour off the page in
floods, and we don't know how to swim in oceans of ink or how to wade
through the drowning that comes from the weight of

/alone/.

We weren't built for this. We weren't built for this.

THERE'S TWO I'S IN SUICIDE
Emily Perkovich (@undermeyou)

I decide I want the whole bottle
I decide I do not want water
I decide to take them one at a time
I will tongue them, one by one
I will swallow dry
I have been here before
I kiss chalk outlines, open-eyed
I kneel before sunset plastic
I stumble through my head
I have been here before
I know this doesn't work
I am supplicant at my own funeral
I wish for the days of belief and placed blame
I wish for the safety of an idol
I hold all of the small ways we grieve alone
I hold back the breath pressing at the back of my throat
I am full of me, again
I have been here before
I decide to drink the water

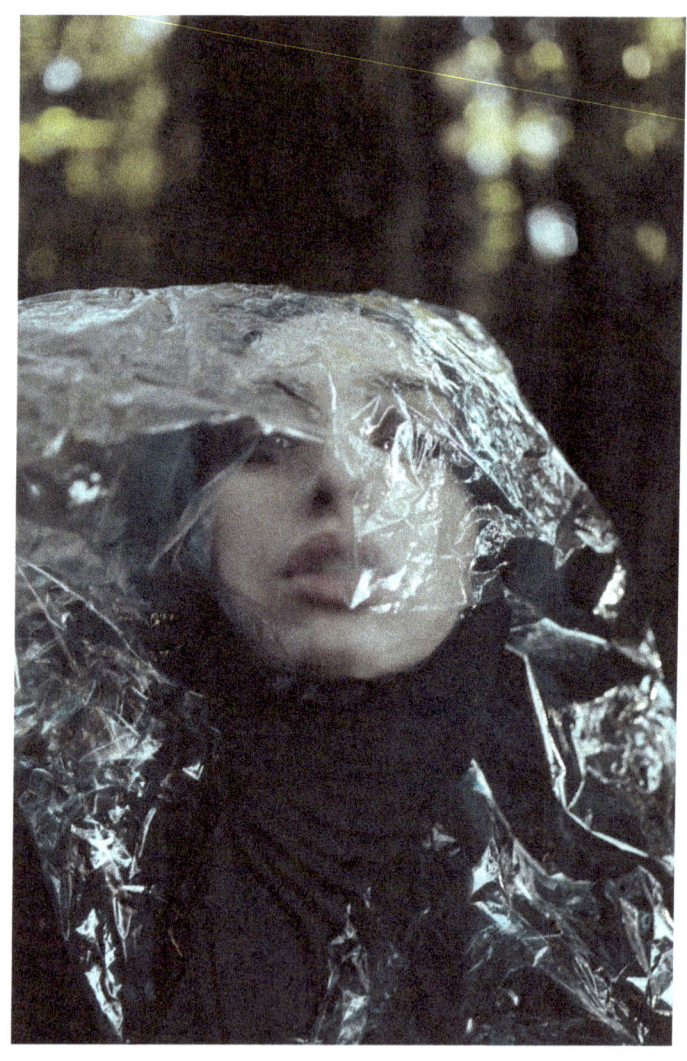

PLASTIC (1 OF 3)
Hanna Webster (@queencortisol) Photography.

STARVING
Emma Morgan (@emmorpoetry)

Does it reside in my belly or my head?
The creature which claws at the fingers,
which long to place sugar on my tongue.
A vacant and bellowing empty thing,
reaches up along my oesophagus,
erupts sickeningly from my mouth,
silently shoves the morsels out.
Signals tripping in my brain,
firing on and off all day. Calculating;
what we can do without? Stills my
hands from hunter gathering.
Together, plan and scheme
my fate. A dull looming ache from
down below, and the quivering
starving Me, inside my mind.

NO BREAD

Emma Morgan (@emmorpoetry)

Found a note, an amuse bouche
from the past, named: *No Bread.*
Hungrily I unwrapped to taste
what morsels I'd laid out;
a list of mundane foods, each accompanied
by a   dash   of   *No.*

No? Oh.
          Oh, no no no.
Insides seize, freeze, try to
appease an old, younger me.
Dragged back to that hollow
space, where my belly and
I, were all out of   pace.

Deny deny deny.
Still don't know precisely why, or
how? Things got quite so a   wry.
Didn't think it was a nutritional
problem. Could have picked a
worse   'coping mechanism'.

Nobody raised it, helped starve
insatiable guilt. Even wolfishly uttered,
          bony limbs would lovely to paint...
Until - you   stared with blatant
fright. Lit skin with harsh daylight.
Nowhere left to hide.

Turned a corner, from the   edge
of danger. Filled and filled and kept
on filling, willing every savoured mouthful to
remain in. Waiting patiently to satiate you.
To thank and feed and pour all over you.

Yet.   Life had come and overtook you.
While I was busy self-indulging, ful-
filling, finally   living. You were
winding down, to dying. If only
I'd have got there sooner, would
your plate have felt any fuller?

Now feast on shame; was my greed
a slice of the blame? And undeservingly,
I taste -   at the placemat across from me;
the richest voice that no longer speaks,
softly willing me to   *eat.*

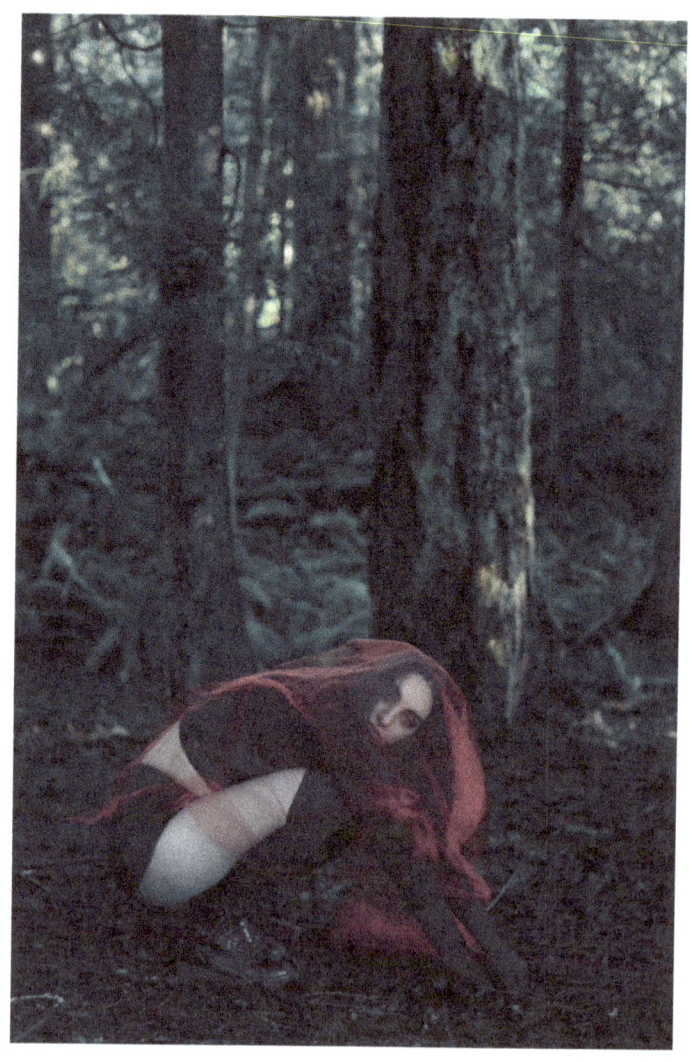

RED (2 OF 3)
Hanna Webster (@queencortisol) Photography.

THEY TOOK THE VOICE I ONCE HAD
Emerson Craig (@ghostofaboy_)

they took the voice i once had
until my wolfish heart trembled compliantly
my veins could smell the bishop in his death
his penance drowning me, mute.

they cut my tail at the root, a hunting trophy.
abandoned in the imminent night,
now without moonlight, a shiver ripples across my skin
unable to resist the futile contortions.

not once did the lunar mother kiss me goodnight
even though i had confessed to her my mortal sin.
& without knowing how to strike a god,
i fell blindly to my knees beneath her translucent rays.

they took from me the childhood i deserved.
lying in the orchard amongst the coyotes,
their howls warned me of monstrosity,
their eyes taught me the tranquility of solitude.

let me live between the pines;
with nascent paws i found sanctuary.
i will never again know the celestial plane,
but maybe one day i will relieve myself of their whispers.

imagine that you are a wandering wolf,
howling to a rock in the distant sky
that won't gift you even the briefest of glances.
would you not also prostrate yourself before the darkness?

with tongue tied to the tail of a comet,
swallowing the promises of an enchantress,
i no longer wish to know their false sermons
that wave me aside without any thought.

& so i have suffocated at last, mother moon,
with tail caught between my cracked lips.
you had wanted me to be your disciple,
but instead received the corpse of a wolf.

THE MOURNING DOVES SING TO US
Emerson Craig (@ghostofaboy_)

the ghost of a boy who once lived in my chest has now grown. he
has enveloped my body, taken control over my limbs, my tongue, sees
through my eyes, smiles when you call my — his — name.

we walk through the streets, alone, but together. he fidgets under the
warmth of the mid-morning sun, not yet used to existing in the daylight.

even so, he gazes wide-eyed at the world around him. he has been
afraid of the light for so long that it will take some time getting
used to it. he whispers in my ear that the leaves of the trees
look different, that the grass peeking through the cracks in sidewalks
seems livelier — everything seems livelier, brighter, happier.

i'm happier, he says through the lump in our throat. i'm happier
than i've ever been. thank you.

i shake my head. thank you, i say. thank you for being willing to
part ways with the dark to join me, here, where your bones are
more fragile and your heart more vulnerable.

he laughs—we laugh. the morning doves sing to us, good morning.

SEPTEMBER 7, 2018

Gabrielle Vaigneur Wheatley (@gabriellevaigneurwheatley)

I do not drink
In the month of September, for it is the month of your departure
And I can easily see myself
Drowning under bottles of rum and vodka,
Waiting for you to return.

They say it should only take a person ten thousand hours
To master any one skill.
If that is the case—
I should have only taken a year to master the art of forgiving
you—
But it has been three years,
And I am no closer.

Did you consider how you would take your leave?
Did you know it would be raining?
Did you know we would gather like
Lambs surrounding the corpse of a sheep killed by wolves?

There was no funeral.
No last goodbye.
Just a goodwill and a god's speed.
We were expected to just continue,
But continue we could not.

I have not forgiven you
For the stolen lines,
They were meant to be mine.

I have not forgiven myself
For not being where I should.

When we were children we played.
I was seven, you were nine.
We laughed and raced, like children do.

I was eighteen when you left,
You were twenty.
I am older now than you'll ever be.
Still, I feel like the child I was:
Scared and powerless, utterly effete.

There are so many questions that poke at my feet
Like the grass with thorns that we'd run through
Barefoot as children.

You'll remember we didn't know the grass had thorns,
But by the time you're halfway through the yard
You must follow through
And walk the rest of the way with thorns in your feet,
Until you reach the other side.

That is what I must do now:
Walk with thorns in my feet
Until I reach the other side.

WOMAN, UNTITLED

George J Cardy (@george.verses)

I've played martyr; thief; their juries;
Teaser; pleaser and fishwife,
I've swapped cells with unborn furies,
Plunge the wound and lick the knife,

I'm a mother and a daughter,
Both the candle and the burn,
Invisible ink author -
I'm the apple in the worm.

RIPTIDE
George Fisher (@g.fisher.poetry)

feeling like i'm caught
in the riptide
pulling me further away
from the safety of shore

breathwork to relax
trying to change the narrative
change the situation
how can i?

i'm tired, too tired
to carry on swimming...
won't someone notice?
can't they see i'm struggling?

between painful breaths
the empty beach taunts me
as overhead waves threaten
to drown me...

EVENING WALK WITH OCD
Hanna Webster (@queencortisol)

—I felt out of place,
the coral sage
adjacent, a slab of peach stone
coated in neon-green lichen
vivid symbiotic
background noise
for errant thoughts.

How do I get out of my head?
Then, fell under again,
flashed mortal wounds,
breathless wailing, the loneliest I have ever been…

My vision clears; I am in the driveway.
Each step measured,
I now retreat farther from home,
thinking not of you.

Thinking only of one moment:
that is, the acknowledgment of the end
settling into one's body,
irrevocably.

I am unable to climb down from the cliff,
how easily an evening walk can be ruined
by my own body.

And what of the last breaths
of everyone I have ever known?
I must follow that thought until I cannot stand myself.
What of my ancestors' DNA in my bones,
a constant reminder of my eventual dissolution?

Feeling still full of voices,
I walk home,
the sky now, periwinkle
and I am thinking of you,
breathing—

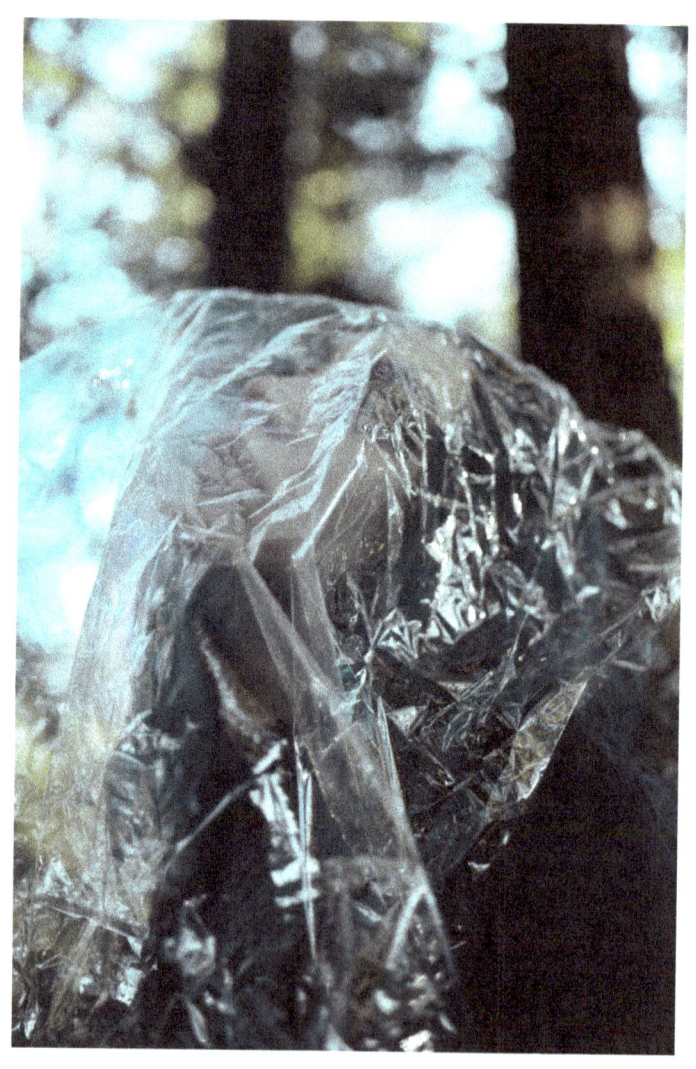

SEARCHING FOR BREATH (3 OF 3)
Hanna Webster (@queencortisol) Photography.

BLUE
Heather C. Moll (@heathercrystalk)

Bound for years within sorrow
she found the deep, fierce blue

guide her away from yesterday
toward this moment, toward

what she held inside. She watched
that blue soak the sky. The horizon

whispered in the distance as day
folded into night. Her body,

dizzy with exhaustion, skin sticking
to skin, desperate to draw a breeze

through the open window. Blue
was the welcome to stars pulling

through the sky every night.
Her eyes longed to witness both,

her own transformation and that
blue drowning the sky.

NO MORE SILENCE
Jai M. Louissen (@bornonadarkmoon)

Unwashed
        draped in frosted burden

   barefooted

beckoned by
        the revenant river

the tree shakes the leaves
   but this nettled curse
      must be plucked
  or it's tendrilous sting will
     take root in milky flesh

a twilight kiss pervades
        unclosing mouth

    sunken

   baptised in valour
verity pours down my thighs
fecund on September reeds

the dogs come for the chase
their snarls slice in denial

Yet I, cloaked in the revenant river
will be silent no more

THE CEMETERY EXPRESS
Joe Rolnicki (@theotherjoerolnicki)

i.

the cemetery express is the next best thing
when your existence splinters to
smithereens
and the sky's ivory divides to black.
steam pipes spike out exhaustive sighs
while the roaring locomotive cries to the
cadence of your calamity.
dreamboat
seascapes wait at the rail's tail and
steel sails call for
abandon
of a tempestuous
dimension

ii.

and your restless suspension spells as the
cemetery express
swallows town
in a surround sound march
to drown out the static of your
personal jury's marathon deliberations.
an offer to flee the futile volley
of a frankensteined grind through
alarm clocks and oil changes
and a thigh-high
supply of
bondage
compilations

iii.

the cemetery express is the inchoate approach
to undo the dismay of unrequested flesh
across calendars of pandemics
and patriarchy -
against the backdrop of a trafficked earth
kidnapped by bootstrap capitalists and
ragtag tycoons who mellonball
a planet's purity to churn out
this year's slate of forgotten car commercials.

oceans of snow and cloud incite covers to
smother nature into
extinction
and you see the cemetery express
arrive in time to leave these
soon-to-be-ruins
for good

iv.

amira the engineer steers the beast toward me.
she sighs with a sneer, piercing.
the daughter of a pirate choir and siren's sea is
weary, clearly tired of my inquiring.
"you again?!" she smirks. "still flirting with
deliverance
or did you miss me?" and pats the seat with the
best view before eye-rolling my hesitation.
"come now. polishing brass can't be this thrilling.
haven't gotten your fill of warning signs,
or do you fetishize the rush from precipitous declines?
we all know you're unfit for loyalty so why see
this through?"
the cemetery express whistles at my waffling
and amira the engineer invites with a stare
that reduce my like to
stone

v.

"the equation-
it's balancing. you've seen that, no?
I'm more honest now. still the prologue to a kinder
story...too much chaos to shake off.
yet, i think of you
at new heights, when a drop is the next stop in our
order of operations;
you never told me the fall gets longer each time.
darker.
i think of you, the impermanence of improvement,
the lure of an invitation to disabuse illusions.
and the futility of individuals
seeking correction
in a house seeping toxic
after each inspection."
amira the engineer sits in the station,
awaiting emancipation from plight

vi.

"what a chore it is – listening to your misery.
and isn't your rock's pre-apocolypse getting a bit
list-y?
take back your fate in a flash
and leave wrath for the wretches
who scorched the path.
your rendition is begging for a reboot.
how many nudges and night stands do you have to see -
you'll never be as complete as you were at 23?"
amira the engineer is getting more personal but doesn't
grasp what worries me.
which means…neither do I. not yet.
"this plane is suffering but I'm not seeking an escape
hatch as much as a superpower or an eleventh hour
where I let my ego go for good. and 23-year-old me has
been dead for a decade. he smiled more but his motives
were stashed in sashes and his personality was a purple
drawstring hoodie"

vii.

"no, what worries me is…
how many revivals do I have left?
I must have chewed through my allowance
by now.
certainly, you and the universe don't owe me
a brightside but will any mammoth insight
stop me from seeing you?
I thought I got it right this time…
how did you find me?
why rise
only to fall
and hear you call my name?
or are your visits just part of the schedule,
regardless of my alignment?
and, and…"

viii.

and the cemetery express rides off again,
lapping past boneyards for thrones and
lavishings.
amira the engineer blows off steam in
streams of a sailor's vocabulary.

her ledger will note a new refusal to board
the inviting, sliding doors, like liner notes
show at 17 or 22 or 26 or 28 or 31 or 33.
"still too curious," she'll write.
but amira the engineer will reappear,
as she always does,
to serenade me with salvation.
until then,
all I can do is resurrect trajectory, pioneer
reason and decry the pull of a siren's
locomotive

PAIN THE PICTURE PRIMITIVE
K. M. Crane (@k.m.crane)

In the morning
it starts
neat and orderly,
the line of needs,
one after the other
and none are yours.

And by the afternoon,
all order is gone,
howls call the pack,
sing feral melody.

Bone boiled stories
told by fire light,
shadow written on walls,
the story of hungry,
hungry need.

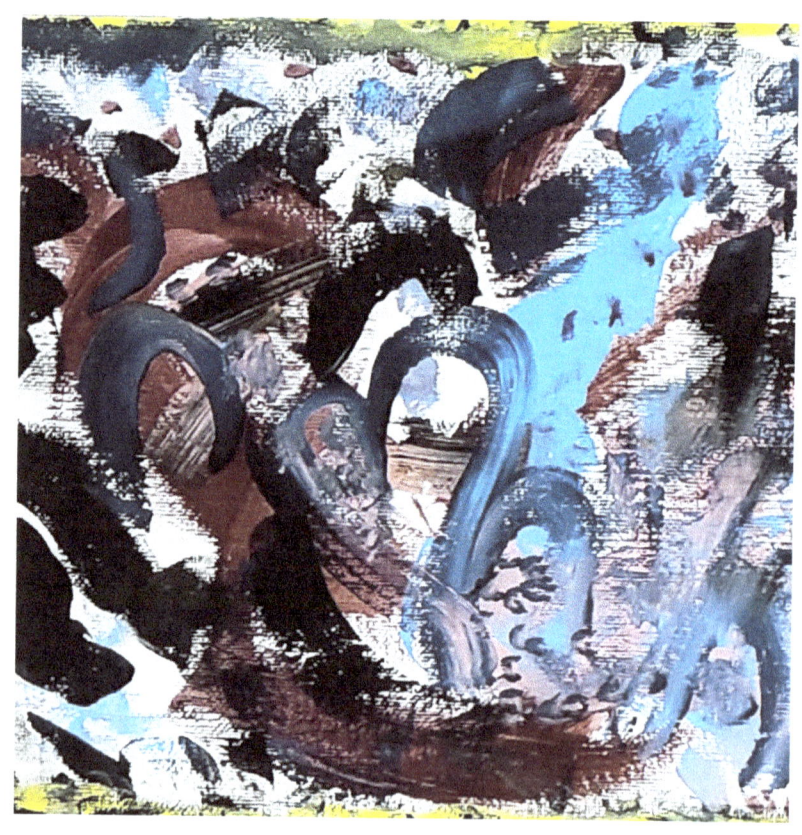

GRIEF
Joan S. Green (@joan.s.green)
October 2021. Acrylic.

MAN MADE MONSTERS
Kate MacAlister (@kissed.by_fire)

I am
a woman
    of sighs
and science
I measure
analyse
consider
all
the possibilities
written among atoms
barely quivering
into existence
I give
flesh
and breath
to the Deep Blue Horror
nesting in the
crooked angles of my smile
and the fractures below

assuring you : *I am just fine.*
it is harvesting
eating away
at my light
with precision and
acute
accuracy
the name is
carefully chosen
for such a Beast
I tend to forget

PHALLACY
Kate MacAlister (@kissed.by_fire)

the year
I found my feet
finally learning to
dance
the world ended

what a lesson
unlearnt
shoving dead weight
of my chest
passing mirrors
and seasons
I wait
I wait ever so
feverishly
for something
to be
drawn
right out

beneath my skin
already shedding
only to see
Mary's monster runs
on coffee
and
an air of
fatalistic optimism

faltered
folded up masquerade
sewn up
Beauty Queens
of circular hells
longing to go
Home

I FEEL GOOD SOMETIMES
Katerina Bacher (@kbacherinawrites)

I feel good sometimes – yellowpetaled and summer breezy   dandelion fuzz
and warm sandy scalp

I feel good sometimes – melted cheesy gooey fingers   wind   scraping   hair
feet hard concrete featherlight sky and*I*

feel good sometimes – shrieking hall empty echo   sound without stop   without
swallow   hands flexing   veins bulging   your ribs a cave   a cavein   your
throat and*yourthroatand*   your fingers   a knife*I feel*

good sometimes – empty at the foot of the bed   hair tied back   shaking
knees toilet cradle   fingers cold   – they're no one's*theyrenoones*   but
yours*I feel good sometimes*taring up at leaves   watch them change   s l o   w
a burst   of warm color   a spin   a riot

I feel good sometimes – hard candy clacking   back of teeth   tongue
music swallow heartbeat wing   slot finger by finger   into someone else
's hand   just be*justbejustbe* something new   someone   new

I feel good sometimes*good sometimes* – I do

YOU COULDN'T SHAKE THIS
Katerina Bacher (@kbacherinawrites)

*you couldn't shake this
if your life depended on it,*
you think, swaying in time
with the squeal of the train,
the words bitter and red
in your throat.

ain't that just how it goes?
the heat of your hand
steams the metal of the pole,
an upright raft keeping you afloat
as the demons
start their daily commute—
crouched backward on benches;
sweeping around poles
like Santa Fe;
crooning paramaniac tunes
in the echo of the metro station,
little clawed hands creasing
the crows of your tired eyes;
teeth not sharp enough for blood,
but enough to hurt
when they sink into you,
enough to hold when
the car shakes, and you feel
your coat swing with it,
river stones sewn into the hem.

the brakes screech again,
and you smile a blunted smile,
because ain't that just how it goes?
ain't that how like calls to like?
a body, a coat,
and a one-way track,
racing each other
to the end of the line

yes, you think,
brakes hitting, doors closing,
car shaking all around you,
that is just how it goes.

A QUIET CRUSHING
Katie Ness (@ katie_wild_yogi)

Sixteen years and a day,
The spell was cast, my heart blistered.
Stinging, scalding. Scattered.
like broiling, boiling blood skies,
A heady broth of volcano-mouthed spite.

There is no way back from this.
The air is raw with screaming, hot shouts of rain,
An empty North Star brightness of loving you,
Clear- Appalling, a smudge of trembling cherry blond light,
You are cut throat, trying to convince me of your prophecy.

In the whirring dissonance, I scratch your words off my soul.
Single breath of Plutonian rancour,
A language riddled with a very red, very wrong universe,
Rapture, rupture, repent.
I am not guilty of the storms.

I am a solar system of soothing, spiralled shells,
Fragile injury of faultline memories.
Ophelia shivered in the beaten earth, sonorous sorrow.
Sprung grace in the undertow, a soft note on a stretching song,
Kissing the chaos back into the image of a deer.

You knew exactly how to deliver hurt. Blue hail eyes.
I sang hymns and buried poppets to erase what you said,
This is the charm of the dog-star bursting,
Tideland breaking into the shape of you; a quiet crushing.
The immortal beauty of becoming maelstrom strangers.

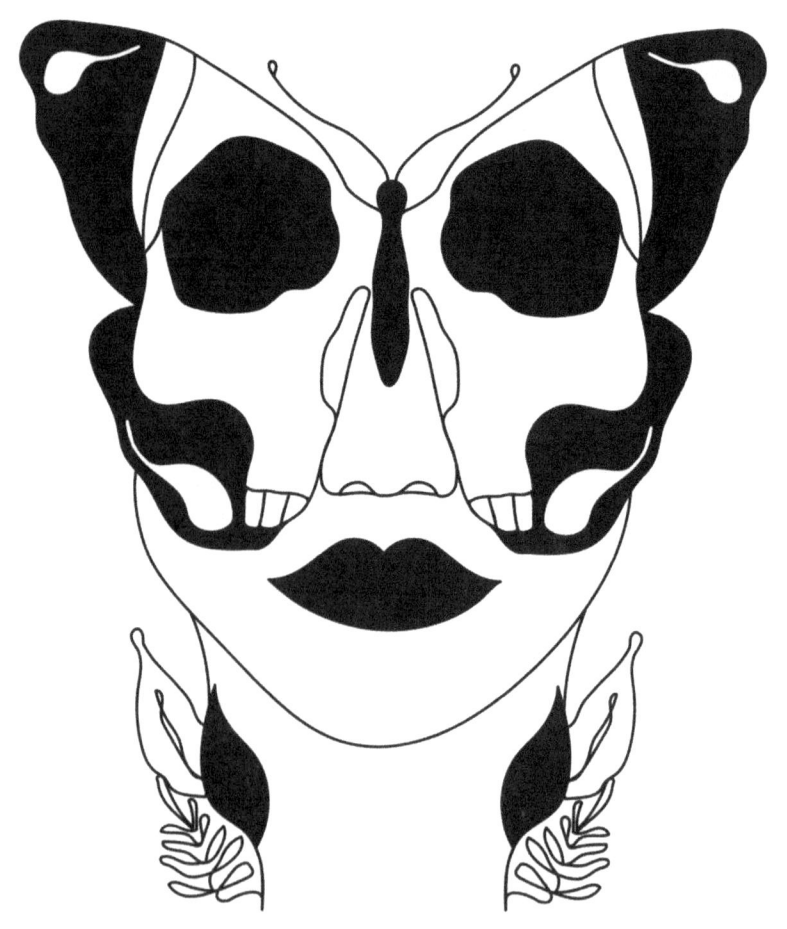

DEADLY FLUTTER
jeganmones (@ jegan__mones) Digital.

BEAUTIFUL METAMORPHOSIS
Katie Ness (@ katie_wild_yogi)

Every night I die
When I think of you,
Small beam and a heartbeat
with no name.
Wondering in the soft twilight,
If you're in the light.

River of red memories,
Hand on stomach,
No one is home.

Every day I live,
You float away
And grow in a distant galaxy.
Astronomical grief,
Calm yet devastating,
But; it's quite beautiful…

RETURN TO WORK
Kris Kaila (@krisesque_life)

I listen,
I watch,
but sometimes I can't take   it   all   in.
Details,
I once revelled in, thrived at
diss i pate once the fog
                    rolls
            in
and the anxiety sets
            roots.
I am in this tunnel

Looking ahead,
straight
in front of me,
I can feel the noise,
            the busyness —
vibrate
palpitate
buzz…zzzz —
sparkling distractions that
take me
away from my
                    next
                            step,
so it is reflex as I
                    walk -
                            stomp
in what feels like
thigh high
sludge
slow
sloppy
— but with purpose.
I hear my name…or is it my name?
Should I stop?….do they need help?
Do they think I am self
-absorbed, self
-fish?
These thoughts
 float
like bubbles, each
l e t t e r
at
a

time –
like the ra-ta-ta of a typewriter,
it takes time to filter, to

comprehend.
And, now I am too far —
I can't turn back.
Or can I? Should I?
Have I stopped?

Or am I still moving?
I'm trying to catch this rainfall
of marbles
that roll
          cascade away from me.
In a maze of people, I feel so
alone — nothing to anchor me,

lead me. Screams
in a language I forgot to practice
has all the answers if I
can
          piece it
together.
Running on this treadmill
my brain is exhausted —
But not a quitter —
just keep calm and carry on.
Carry on as if everything is normal
as our world drowns itself

in opulence, shaking off the rules
for all, "but not for me!"
Carry on as if you didn't actually ask for aid
— when help was offered,
"don't struggle on your own" —
then shrugged off as it cannot
be all fixed by
fucking lunch time yoga.

MY LIFE IS A NEVER-ENDING LOAD OF LAUNDRY
L.A. Roquemore (@loveisanaction)

my weary bones beg for rest
between loads
lower back presses against
familiar cold metal curve
i feel the vibration up my spine
water filling the drum

shrieks of my children
drowned out
by mechanical sounds
spinning, clanking, whirring,
filling, washing, kneading, drying;
zippers and buttons.

this: the
soundtrack of my life.
these:
the stifled tears,
long, tired exhales,
through downturned lips.

in these stolen moments i find
The Last Shred Of My Sanity
tucked away.
i keep it next to the rolled ball of lint
sitting atop a tub
which once held coffee, in
a previous life.
now, it
holds
little lost things:
other shreds
waiting to be claimed:
once beloved pocket rocks,
carabiners, brass keys which tested
every lock they met,
a lone plastic pocket grenade,
a single, silver collar stay.

i visit these signs of life,
eyes pressed tightly shut
looking against the same
dark lids
of all my years
for signs
of who I once was
before
I forgot myself
before I forgot
what rest is
before
seconds of leaning
against a washing machine
became my safe haven.

I JUST WANT TO TURN OFF THE LIGHTS. AND CEASE TO EXIST.

L.A. Roquemore (@loveisanaction)

i don't know what happens next, anymore. i saw my own Death today like i haven't before; i felt its longing like i haven't, before. i stood in the kitchen, daydreaming Death. metal against flesh pulled the trigger BURST out of this Body this frozen Body. i stood, holding onto the oven door handle, stuck in place, eyes unblinking, heart pounding. fluid of my grief all down my face and neck, in my shirt, snot on my lips
i   AM   NOT   R E A L L Y H E R E

This Seems A Different Kind of Panic Attack.
i feel like i am dying. i feel like i'm half gone. minutes pass by, Blood red digital blocks on the oven clock. i hear my world without hearing it at all. i even answer my name being called i help without thinking. i run on fumes. ointment on bug bites, snacks opened, cleanup done, all while running on Empty (*i wonder about fumes.*)

Sylvia Plath Put Her Head In An Oven.
in my mind's eye, i longed for a cold blade to slice flesh. i closed my eyes; i imagined it. (*i remembered it, from another life.*) i saw blood pouring from cuts in my legs; longed for it to drip down my wrist. at the thought, chills went through me; warmth, too. i just want to escape. i wish I could time travel...

GO. BACK.
since i can't, i would like to prevent any more Forward Motion. i'm frozen here in the present, in agony. this is why i run away (*from my Feelings*) when they catch up, i can't breathe. *i can't breathe; i wish i never had to take another breath.* one wound touches another. there are so many versions of me (*that i remember*) to hate (*only when my Feelings catch up to me*) i must just keep moving forward. so i don't Die. and so i Die as soon as possible. both are true; this mutually exclusive mindfuck of existing.

run. on empty. on fumes. on anything.
i distracted myself from daydreaming Death; googling which statistic i would become: Women poison themselves more than men. Men use guns more than women.

it seems the older you get, the more likely to die (by your own hand) holding a firearm. i gathered information because I'm scared, and i do that, when i'm scared. math is in everything. statistics disappear personhood. in this way, i died without dying, in this way i got my feet on the ground again. gathered myself to lock all the knives in the lockbox. built little walls, roadblocks between weapons and the flesh of my children's mother. i am scared to find something, to save me.
and i am scared that this darkest day yet will be the end.

i don't know who to reach for

i don't want more suicide to touch *the one who lost her dad this way*
i don't want *the ex* to blame himself more than he should
i don't want more tragedy for *the one who worked to be light*
i don't want *the one who can't sleep* to lose another night
i don't want *the one who's too busy* to question if she had made time
i don't want ███████ or ██████ or ████ or anyone
to drop everything
i don't want *the ones who are resting* to regret taking a vacation.
i don't want my children lost, unable to ever reconcile their origin story.
i don't want *my sister* to ache
i don't want *my parents* to swallow my memory, a swill of bitter regret.

i don't want *my people* to carry my ghost, a heavy vapor. i don't want
my pain to rehome itself in their bones.

I Just Want to Turn Off the Lights & Cease to Exist
Without Causing Anyone Else Pain.

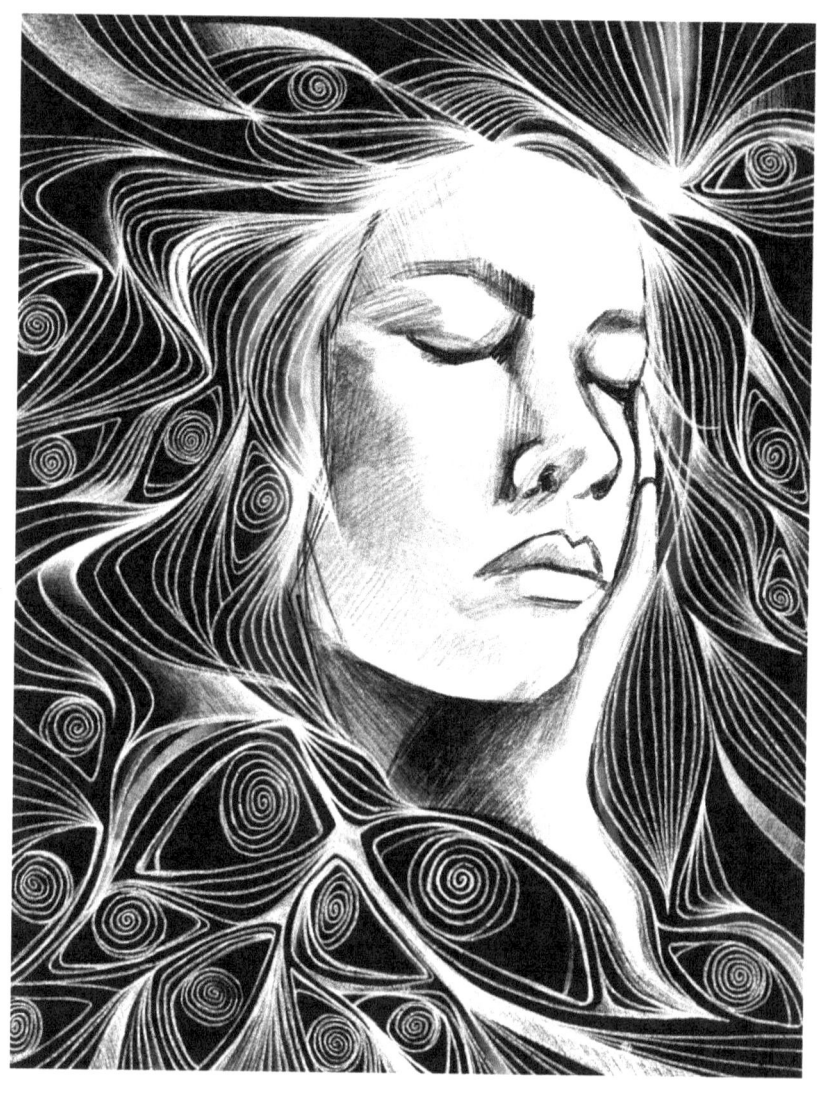

REST
Olivia Zhang. Digital.

BREAKFAST COMPANION
Lee Hodgins / Spellwriter (@spellwriterpoetry)

"People were crazy with pain and secrets." - Anna Funder

It came up on me a warning wrapped
    in a promise--forming my changes--an
ache of early death bridged
    by winter lightning this future-

present strain bug-eyed
    at the kitchen table picking
      claustrophobic scabs opening the bleed--
tongue out slow motion burrowing and waiting.

There is no dancing in this
    funeral dress fingering tablecloth
    fantasies hung without a care in the panes
of windows that mourn the loss of grieving, I

am bargaining, to split the
    difference between a lie and a
hoax--sipping amphetamines starving
    on platitudes spilled from infected lips.

The pink moon, disguised as peace, spies
    on me carrying the stones of
my family's home--shouldering the legacy
    of their shadows I am the misfit rock, and

now I understand--an immaculate mind affords
    no cover in petulant times and I am that
person back of the carton missing face
    unidentified in what remains of me.

The sky is reckless sweat, I fall into its
    night for a hundred straight days--no fucks
given--resolve turning against me as it
    lies twitching in the corner of my eye, the
ground beneath is an injury clawing back its
    measure of debt and, I'm ashamed to tell you
how I try digging for hope, accidently
wringing it to death in my hands.

In the end I am the full frontal
    co-confessor--splayed and tied to
      the stake of winter
  conspiracies filling the heads of cannibalized tin
        soldiers, spilling their tea on
    the battlefields of
      social hysteria.

This spring there will be no
    coriander bloom only reverence
         for the passing crowds and
      solitudes upon solitudes.

1X RECYCLED PRAYER INCOMPLETED BY SILENT AMENS

Lucas Pearce (@lucas.pearce)

time is our devil unprejudiced
i shed a tear for the befores
then another for the afters
which is to say none go
to soon they go on the
same whim a newborn
cries

i write these words with less
feeling than last time prayers
live in the heave of my
chest i offer breath in
their memory i wish
us all better peace

AFTER I DID NOT DIE
Lucas Pearce (@lucas.pearce)

the road brooded at near-motorway speeds,
brooded in nigh-coffin black, tar close enough
i could almost smell it. mother held
my arm. i unbelted & aimed for the oncoming
car, door open like a seraph's wing. my brother
howled as if fear would keep me still.

i did not die.

starry reverie outshot lightspeed-suicide
agenda. i saw hints of heaven & hell fire
disco-lighting the windscreen. the universe
condensed itself into an open mouth,
the shrill of tyres marking road, a squint-worthy
sky – a warrior heaved me to her chest.
my brother had emptied his lungs
of all sound, save his breath.

i did not die.

& yet i had gazed at that of which
i was mortally ineligible. my heartbeat
trespassed inside my body's arenaceous
halls; encroached like persephone's
pomegranate swallow.

in the chill of night my bones would
rattle query:

does gazing on
heaven
not demand
sacrifice?

i gave it fear, & taught myself
to pretend in the company of others
that i did not know death's face
as a friend.

because i did not die.

THE FETISH DREAM WAS NOT ABOUT BÉLA LUGOSI—
THAT WAS A DIFFERENT DREAM

Lynne Ellis (@stagehandpoet)

You came to me brighter than
that dream where teeth
crumble-crunch like porcelain
and fall into my hands.
I've not had that dream
for nine years, never since
a boozed-up driver busted
my jaw and a surgeon
screwed the fragments
to titanium chain link.
I lost four teeth on scene,
one cracked in half
and one leaned left
until the nerve gave up, so
now I dream of pliers
and procedure chairs.

I spent the night with you,
these visions dulled in their holes.
You pulled my hair back
in fistfuls, called me worthy.

Béla Lugosi came to me
in a dream, whispering,
"Your body is empty spaces
filling other empty space."
On waking I looked
for those spaces and found
them all whole—like when
your scent holds to the bandana
in my back pocket so I hold it
to my lips at intervals all day—
hands no longer full
of blood or bone.
I spent the night with you,
you put clothespins in my hair.
All lit up and wild, I rumbled
where you locked me into leather.

You clipped clothespins to my skin.
All lit up and wild, your breath
came in long draws and you
held me to you at the hip.

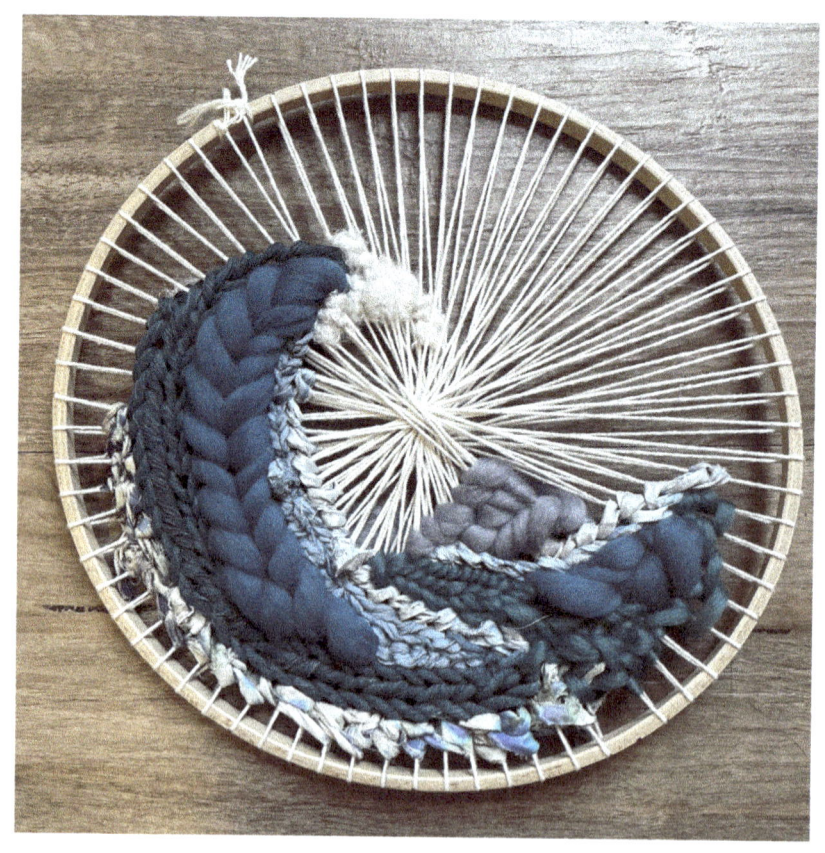

THE WAVE
Melia Donk (@meliadonk) 30cm diameter.
Fabric, wool, string, bamboo.

URCHIN DAYS
Madison Gill (@sweetmint_poet)

On urchin days my nerves sharpen
into fine black points, poke from my skin
like razor grass. You pull away, and everywhere
I touched your body is dotted with red –
my venom spreading. I was only trying
to hold you, too. Beneath this hard-shell armor
is a creature softer than an egg yolk,
and it is so afraid. And who can blame it?
When I have carried it with me into the mouths
of too many alligators already. Now it lashes
out at the slightest semblance of closing jaws,
even an embrace. I know I can't protect it,
but I try anyway. I worry if I relax my fist
for one second, it will fall out of my hand
onto the floor. Then the thing I can't see moving
in the shadows will close in and lap its delicacy
from each kitchen tile. And what if I can't endure
that kind of pain? So sit with me here, beside the window,
while I filter the light through my bristles.
After a moment, my hands will become hands
again. Your wary touch in the dimple
of my back softens all my sharp ends
into dandelions. The kind with a tiny cloud
at the end of each stem – a bouquet of feathered
wishes. I make the same one on all of them:
that you never resent me for this ritual.
That you stick around through the growing
I still have to do. One day I'll be all petal
and no thorn. You will walk through the garden
of me in awe of my blooming masterpiece –
the result of your patient watering

MAELSTROM
Madison Gill (@sweetmint_poet)

The mind is a beast
we are all tasked
with taming

but how?

When mine ducks every lasso
throws me from the saddle
kicks dirt in my mouth.

Is named for the ocean's
blood riling beneath
the throbbing bruise of sky –

\thunderheads colliding
like clashing gods
threatening a slaughter of rain.

One second I am holding
the reins. The next
I am a torn sail

hanging from a splintered mast
swallowed by a wall of water black
as my most poisoned thoughts.

I am sinking like a pearl
to the shifting tectonic floor
of my own body

drawing breath
through a mouthful of sand.
My pruning hands

bound behind my back
by mangled leather.
But reins cannot tame the sea.

EPILEPSY
Marc Brimble (@marc.brimble)

I understand

I am
  falling,
my hands
grabbing and grasping
find no   purchase.
all around me
is smooth
     and slippery
beneath my feet
     a running river.
– in this instant
     time becomes unmoving –
each soundless moment
un
 -mistakable
       and   lucid
and
I realise
     I can't

stop.

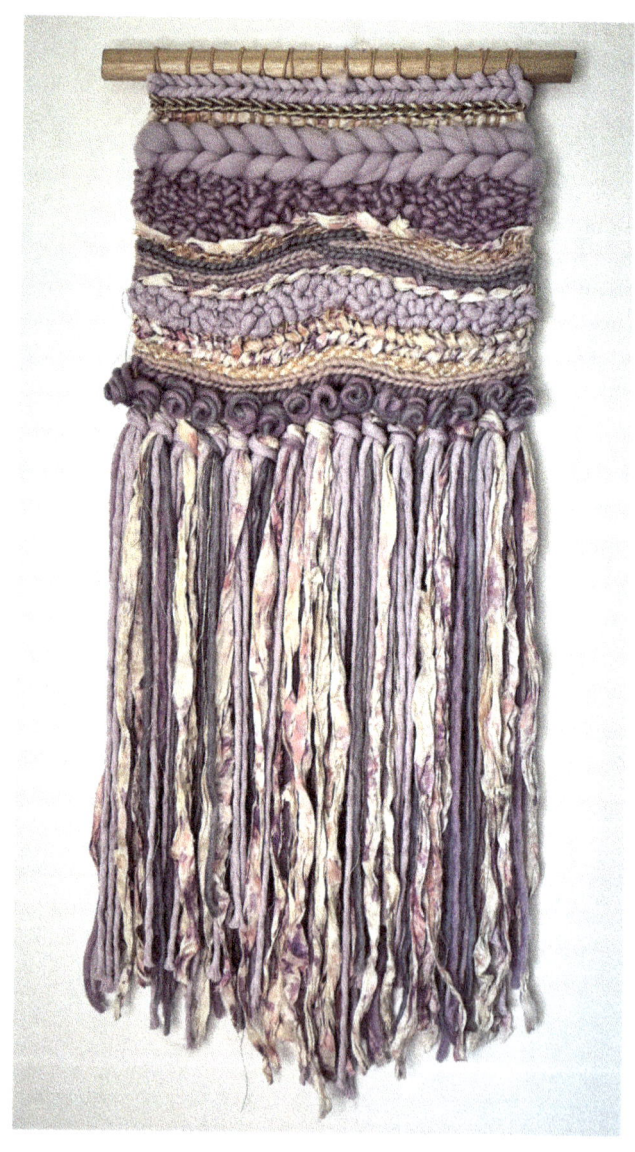

LAVENDER TEA
Melia Donk (@meliadonk) 33 x 77cm.
Fabric, wool, string, bamboo.

UNDO
Myheart_poetry (@Myheart_poetry)

How to undo you from me
   The passion
   The trauma
   The ache

My throat tightens
   Dancing flames
   Lured by sultry smoke
   Wax scalds as it spills

My breath catches
   Burnt birch
   Hollowed from the inside
   Ash crumbles at the touch

What was once divine
   Eviscerated
Rusty shards
   Pierce every longing
   Dreams twisted into pain

Pulled out of time and space
   My body
     Mind
     Heart
   Are under your control
     Again

The memories stronger
   Than reality
     Could ever be

THERE ARE NO GOLD STARS
Naomi Head (@naomieah)

There are no gold stars when you're a grown up.
There's no participation award for getting out of bed
or buying groceries, not even when you remember
to eat the leftovers from last week's batch cook.

There are no gold stars when you're a grown up.
It doesn't matter how many emails you send,
how many followers you have, whether you trend,
or how many spices you hoard in the kitchen drawer.

There are no gold stars when you're a grown up.
No credit for cleaning the hair out of the drain,
no certificate for emptying the bin, and no trophy
for another job regularly forgotten but finally done.

There are no gold stars when you're a grown up,
but you can eat chocolate whenever you want.

SPACIOUSNESS
Rachel Dickens (@lollysnow)

The spaciousness,
My brain unspooling,
Tentatively stretches out its roots,
Into the luscious green undergrowth,
The rough and tumble of cobwebs being
swept and stones unearthed.

Shedding my lizard skin, wriggling into
comfort, spreading out webbed digits, back
to the sun.

Unpacking my soul from a suitcase. From tiny
boxes and laying out the contents in
numerous possibilities.

I can choose to put them back or let them
be, see what they become in this new trusty terrain.

And I know the city is disposable,
unforgiving and not missing expendable me.

THE ~~SUM~~ SON OF OUR PARTS

Rachel Dickens (@lollysnow)

Ignite me, set me on fire with little deaths,
When cinders fall, concede us together,
Indelible ink penned out our future,
Residing as ghosts, I hope he keeps us close.

In his attic, your tarnished coffee rings,
Lint on my black mourning gowns,
The crumbling icing feeding the diamond-shaped moths.
Our portraits ageing emotionally,
Gold gilt frames preventing us from spilling out,
Taking over the room with our outpourings.

I wish I could dissect the spores of suffering from you,
Analysis them, capture cloudy breath in a glass jar,
Label it as a reminder,
Not to sigh down to our child.

With oil burning bright, tiny flashlights,
Fill each corner that life doesn't reach.
The soot will form and make pitched poppies.
Our entrails behind us,
We try to stretch our damaged wings in the wind.
Flying high, he is stronger than us already.

MONSTERS IN WAITING
Rainlily (@rainlily)

I succumb to twilight thinking.
all the light and dark things
caught in the in-between,
licking their fangs
like so many monsters,
not having the dignity
to hide under the bed
or slip inside
some long forgotten crevice
where I can pretend
that I don't know
their names.

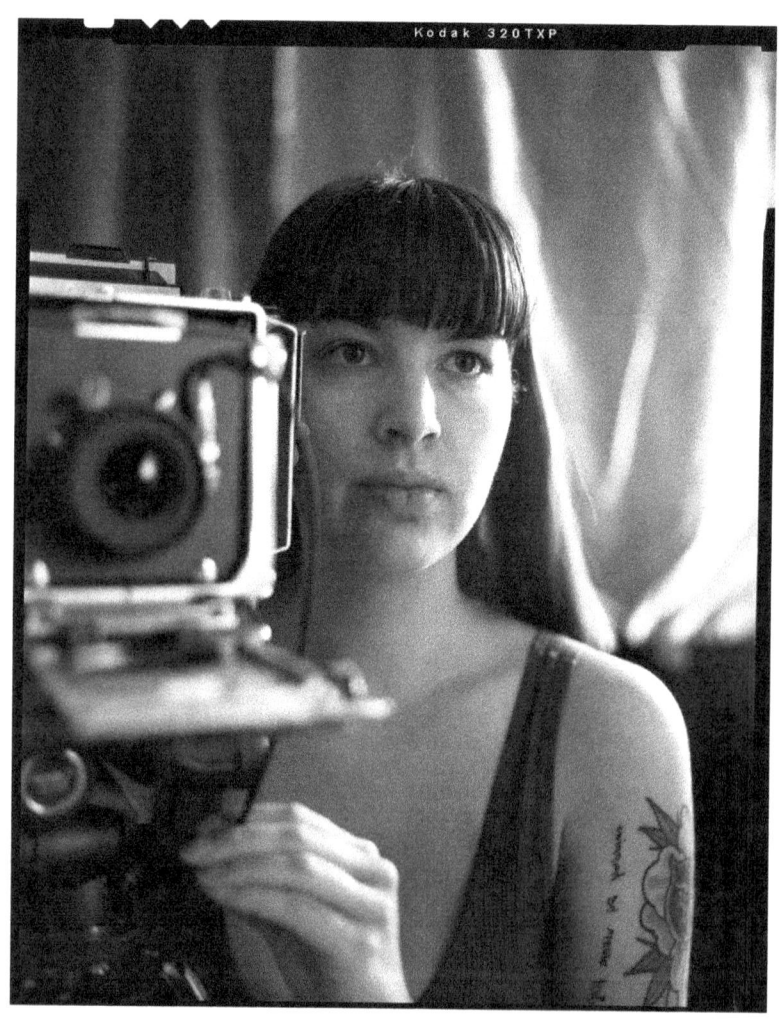

SARAH
Sarah Eckstine (@saraheckstine)
Photography.

SWALLOW ASHES
Rebecca Rijsdijk (@rebeccarijsdijk)

the world is burning
and i am still
crying
about a boy
with two faces
happy to serve
all those who
pay
tribute
with their
words

the world is burning
and i don't get out
of bed until noon
drinking g&t's
in my pyjamas
on a good day
still going to work
to shine for the elderly
who complain
about someone cheating
a game of cards
and did
you see
what mrs
so and so
was wearing
to lunch today

the world is burning
and i eat my way
through a packet
of citalopram
flushed down
with energy drinks
and cigarettes

cleaning up
the human waste
my patients
leave behind
i am a highly
functioning
depressed
piece of
shit
i tell my therapist
she says i have
to be nicer to myself

the world is burning
and my tongue
hurts of all the things
i did not say
to his perfect
little face
i swallow ashes

the world is burning
and so am i

JUST A TAP
Robin Cressman (@robincressman)

I'm used to
injecting drugs

not intravenous;
subcutaneous.

But now there's a needle
sticking out of my back

for some reason.

I feel spinal fluid
leaking out of my lumbar

like just a drop of soul
leaving the body.

One drop rolls down my side
thicker than water

Is this how a maple tree feels
when we tap it for syrup?

Does it give freely,
knowing its sweetness is loved

on pancakes?

That's the only connection
I can make right now

as my soul is tapped
from this body

in drops.

The radiologist was kind
and cute.

His assistant was
a friendly ghost

of a woman

with wide,
pale eyes

like she lives on this planet
but also on the moon.

She commutes.

Like me
between the medical

and the rest of
the world.

IT TRIES TO ESCAPE
Sidrah (@writing.by.SA)

Snap back to my body,
an elastic band still twanging,
blur in and out of focus.
Standing to my left,
thick prisms on my eyes
separate light; everything
has a spectrum outline,
shadow forms, past tense selves
of every wavelength. Blink away
the sevenfold vision but it's too late:
I see the contours of my face fizzing,
grab my hand to pull me back in

> (a risky game being your own anchor,
> might lose your nerve stitching your shadow
> back on).

The stab of healing brings you back sometimes
to where you are, walking on threads.

At least there is friction now,
between the soles of your feet
and the worn carpet,
silhouettes digging their nails in.

Who holds more weight
and if it tries to escape?

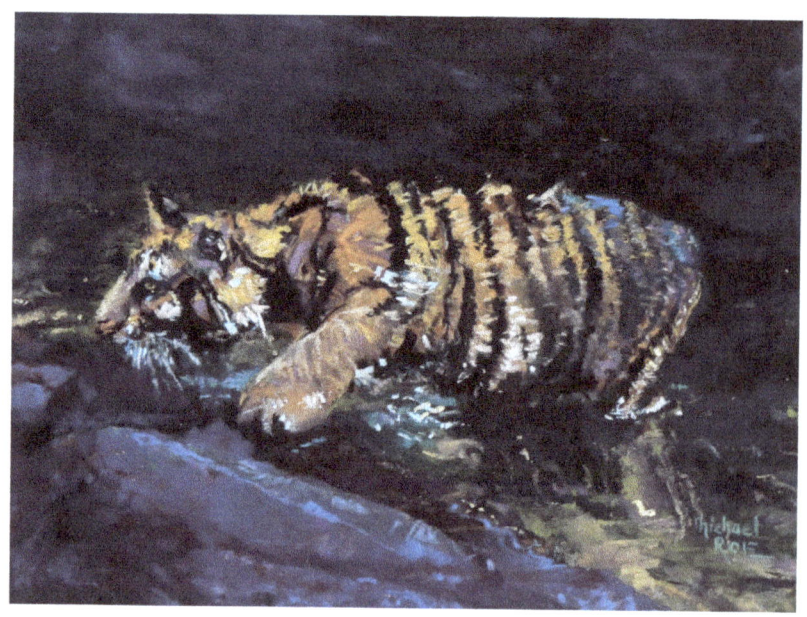

ON THE HUNT
Michael Roe. Pastels on canvas.

WHITEWATER
Samuel Boerma (@samboerma)

Why do you walk into the water
expecting family, expecting a homecoming
instead of the simple taste of salt? we would ask.

And as outside the rain would plummet
straight as light, cold as abandonment, he would say:
Because everything within these tall bones, this white canvas

seems to wash ashore in waves.
Even his hair curled like the crest, like the foam
frothing to cascade over the rock of nose, the banks of lips.

Is it not the only honest answer?
That it all keeps coming indefinitely, but
that each day, each month and each season

have some soft respite balled in their fists?
If music is the silence found between the notes
then life's peace is found between the sets, found

when wind and swell subside;
when swimming becomes returning home
instead of slowly drowning.

SICK (FUCK!)
Simon Hauwaerts (@simonhauwaerts)

The sky today is bluer than the sea has ever been,
bluer than my bottle of mouthwash,
the one I had to replace after throwing & giving up one time too
many
or too few, depending on who you ask
of course. Nothing is self-evident today. It was
yesterday, hopefully will be tomorrow,
but today I can't stop making
comparisons between skies
and mouthwash bottles, used tissues and clouds, skyscrapers
and rusty needles, rusty needles and broken records, unused
condoms and hospital gloves. All hopelessly stinking
of nothing
in particular. Nothing
marinating in nothing until
the heaviness of it all breaks my back and I crawl back
into bed, hauling my body back aboard, waiting
until the sea goes from blue to grey again, until the air stops
shouting, until it all becomes
just
a little less
end
less

TALKING THERAPY
Simon Hauwaerts (@simonhauwaerts)

It's supposed to be a vowel,
the shape of That travelling from my brain
to my tongue going down,
not back down my throat this

time but
down to my fist,
the red red red
therapeutically sanctioned
this time, punching bag ready.
The people next to me all have vowels for
their Thats:
aaaaaaaaaaaaaa! or
even u? or
O! I gather it and try to shape it
into

J. J? Bottle, fire and then j.
that jjjjjjjj

Thajjjjjjjj

Deep breath. My apologies.

It really helps she says. Just jjjjjjjust
aaaaaaaaa

Pow! I try
to
jjjjjjjjjjj

jj

jjjjjjjjjjjjjjjjjjjjjjjjjjjjjjjjjjjjjjjjjjjjjjjjjjjjjjjjjjjjjjjjjjjjjjjjjjjjjjjjjjjjjjjjjjjjjjj
jjjjjjjjjjjjjjjjjjjjjjjjjjjjjjjjjjjjjjjjjjjjjjjjjjjjjjjjjjjjjjjjjjjjjjjjjjjjjjjjjjjjjjjjjjjjjjjj
jjjjjjjjjjjjjjjjjjjjjjjjjjjjjjjjjjjjjjjjjjjjjjjjjjjjjjjjjjjjjjjjjjjjjjjjjjjjjjjjjjjjjjjjjjjjjjjj
jjjjjjjjjjjjjjjjjjjjjjjjjjjjjjjjjjjjjjjjjjjjjjjjjjjjjjjjjjjjjjjjjjjjjjjjjjjjjjjjjjjjjjjjjjjjjjjj
jjjjjjjjjjjjjjjjjjjjjjjjjjjjjjjjjjjjjjjjjjjjjjjjjjjjjjjjjjjjjjjjjjjjjjjjjjjjjjjjjjjjjjjjjjjjjjjj. Sorry.

TEA WITH MY MONSTER
Sophia Mihailidis (@soph.eeah)

There are no clocks here, I apologize
So a while could turn into forever
But I guess we'll never know
Are you hungry?
I have here the hearts of the many you have disappointed
They're still warm, feel them!
They've just stopped beating!
Or perhaps if you're thirsty,
I can make us tea
Brewed from every soul you've toiled over
Spent countless nights crying over
I sought them out especially for you
Do you remember?
Do you remember them?
Why do your eyes keep darting to the door?
Perhaps I should lock it
You see, I very seldom get company
And yours seems to be so welcome
What's your hurry?
Stay!
Stay!
Oh, maybe you'd like to hear my stories?
Of the many miserable days I've spent locked away in my chamber
Tearing at the walls, ripping at my skin
Leaving red raw marks across my body
I apologize for the glass all over the floor
Sometimes, I look in the mirror
And snarl at my reflection
I can't bear to look at myself
So I smashed my reflective surfaces
Am I hideous?
It's okay if you think so
Most people don't like having me around
I suppose it's because of the way I make them feel –
Uncomfortable, as if they could jump out of their own skin
Like ants crawling within them
And then suddenly they throw me out
And I'm back here, alone again
But oh! You've come to me!
Another welcome visitor!
Please tell me you'll stay,
I will make you feel so at home
I'll create a place for us and you will never have to leave

All I ask in return
Is that you give me every single tear
Every bad memory
Every painful thought
Every piece of you that exists
Forever.

I'M WORRIED ABOUT HER

Sophia Murray (@sim_poetry)

Her clam shell eyes are trapped in webs of thin blue veins on coconut milk skin. Single tears stop on the verges of soft pink plump cheeks. She licks the raw top lip. Hands fumble at her throat to pull the words out. Skin is chewed and paper skin pulls off fingernail beds like tiny ghostly sprouting plants that never saw light. Freckles and broken spots dance across the backs of her hands until they rest in each other's embrace. Head to one side, her tongue darts out to the left and pulls an auburn curl in between perfect teeth. She rubs it between her lips like she's just freshly applied watermelon lip balm. And you're afraid to ask what causes this but it's your job. You're afraid that when those chewed strands of hair let the secrets out, that you can't help. You can't fix what has been broken. But you ask because it's your job. And when that string of knots falls out between perfect teeth and each knot has been tied in grief, in violence and in pain, you will sit together silently. Then you split. You splice. You will unfurl each growth. And you know the string will never lie straight again, kinks and waves still pass through on quiet nights, but now it lies around us, carried together, bound.

SILENCE BORN
Susan Niemi (@ slniemi59)

Silence born to her mind,
Tender at age 3, she slipped
Outside her body disappearing
In muted fear, shame, rejection
Of her innocence, sh sh sh.

Her steps brushed like whispers
Footprints fading quickly
Her movements suggested in
The transparent motion of the
Heat rising from the street.

The only evidence of her existence
Was the silence of the sh sh sh
Slamming forward in felt fear, shame,
Rejection. Screaming into nightmares,
At age 34 and 3, body and memories collide.

Silence pried open in ugly, bloody,
Grief, sorrow. Despair. Examined,
Her story was written in my bones
Relived in my cells, the memories
Recorded in my empty brain.

At age 34 and 3 we learned to play
Stomping with gleeful joy, we
Left big little girl footprints.
Wounds healing in illumination
Reuniting towards wholeness.

Silence still lingers sh sh sh
In the fear of rejection, the moments
Of felt shame, of sorrow or loss
Convinced they won't believe.
Muting the joy, hushing my voice

Willfully I will struggle forward
Beginning with whispers and
Words on the page to learning
My voice, supporting myself in my
Stumbles and my triumphs.

At age 60, 34, and 3 I am growing bolder
Willing to face my lingering responses
Of trauma playing at being habits.
Finding belonging, belief, love.
I am loving myself into being whole.

WAVES
Stephanie Farrell-Moore (@stephfarrellmoore)

Those times
when I clung
to the edge
of the seat
secretly
purging
all
of my feelings
dreams
beliefs
the whole
of my grief
get it out
outside of my self
a guilty
cry for help
why didn't I
turn
to scribbled words
and soundlessly
get it down
safely
on to paper
instead of
splashing
bile and
wave after
wave
of sadness
into a bowl
shower full power
for loudness
holding on to
nothing
turning my
soul inside out

the only way
of shouting
but now
I know how
to house
this beast
scrawling her
between sheets
of paper
but back then
for years
and endless
tears and pleading
while pleasing
all the people
that needed her to
she still seemed
entirely
untameable
yet in her head
completely reasonable.

NAP
Troy Turner (@troynturner)

pushing, pulling.
the gentle tide
that is your breath
makes me dizzy
while you sleep.

NAUSEA IN THE WOLF'S MOUTH
Wynnie (@_bashful.violet)

I stopped caring
About the way my body carried its weight,
The moment I realised
That I loved the way it withered when it starved.
The way I loved the feel of each rib
Rippling between hungry fingers.
I stopped caring about the way my body carried its weight,
When I realised that I loved the feel of its struggle
When it could not hold food inside of me.
I stopped caring about the way my body carried its weight,
When I was able to see
That not all wolves are strangers.
That not all diseases are biological.
That society can plant demons inside of you
While telling you they're planting roses.
In that moment,
I pulled the plug on those demons.
I stopped caring how my body carried its weight.
I cut the wolf's throat.
It was a baptism of flesh.
I found salvation in the curves of this body
And I placed love in all the empty spaces
I had ripped from its earth
With hands painted by strangers.

BREATHLESS
Zoe Simmons (@ somethingbeginningwithz)

Breathe—

It's hard to.

There's more which
I cannot control
Than
What
I
Can—
And that's okay

Breathe, and cling:
To an idea
To a thought
To a goal of metamorphosis

It gives me strength
When I feel
As if
My body does not

Low energy;
Drained
I cling to your body

Because it feels as though I do not have my own

Control

Give in

There is none.

Only fire.

It glints
Glistens
And shines

And then, I know

Even through the darkness
Even through the raging storms of my mind
I burn

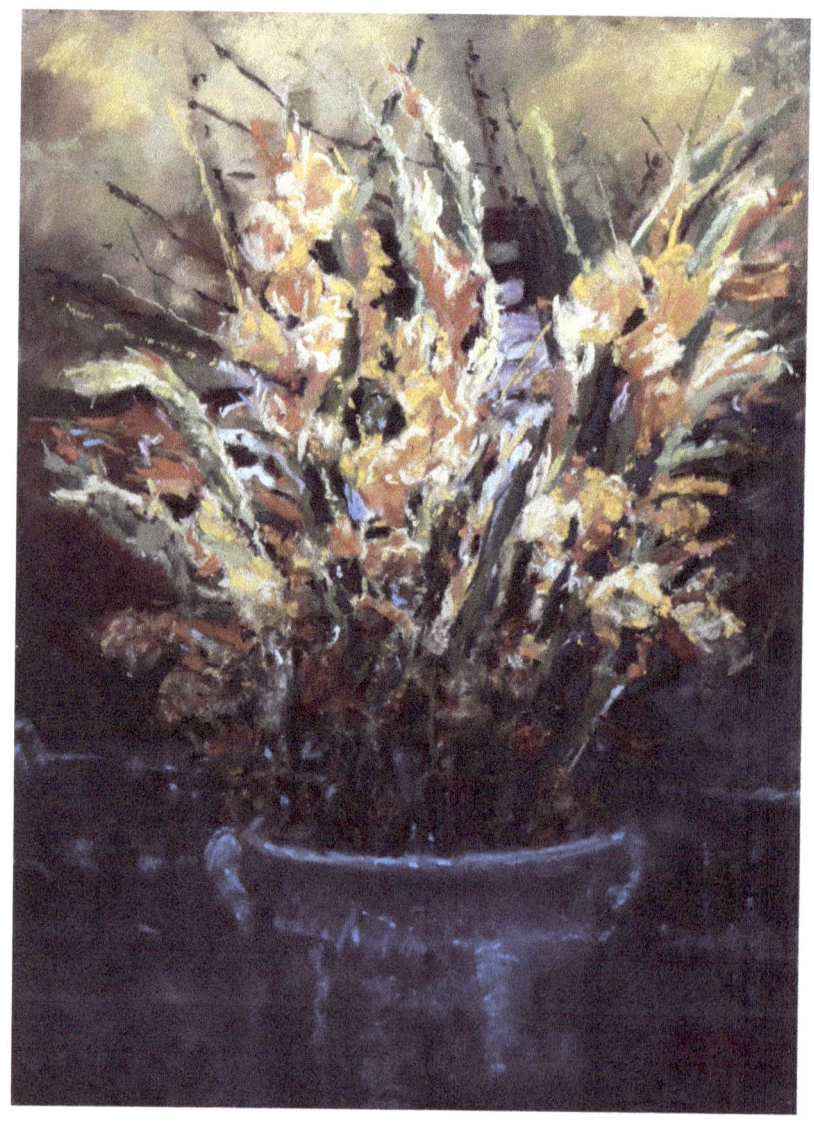

GLADIOLUS
Michael Roe. Pastels on canvas.

STORYTELLER
Zoe Simmons (@ somethingbeginningwithz)

It started with a whisper;
A trickle of essence
Seeping through tiny cracks
In the armour I had made,
Chipping
More and more
With every word.
Every connection
Every story
Every moment of truth
Breaks down cold concrete walls
Unleashing a smidge of the light within.

I fear their reactions when they see me
I want to belong
I want to know myself—truly
Wholly
But I am a mystery
An enigma
Dazzling and dizzying to the mind; my mind
It combusts,
Self-imposed constraints implode
As I too implode
With shattered identity,
Seeking acceptance
Seeking warmth
Seeking understanding;
A sanctuary:
Home.
And speaking out;
Sharing
Brings me one step closer
To
The discovery
Of
Myself

ABOUT THE CREATORS

a.g. (she/they) is a teacher, writer, and artist, born and raised in the middle of nowhere, ohio. their work centers on their experiences as they expound into adulthood, choosing to grapple, celebrate, and honor the countering grief and joy that remains. her work is featured in Sunday Mornings at the River, and their debut poetry collection, "on the edge of enough" is set for release in late 2022. IG: *@written_by_ag*

AJ Wojtalik (she/her) is a writer from Colorado, balancing a day job in marketing while raising a remarkable tween wolf and rambling in nature as much as possible. Her poetry is a reflection of her relationships to self, others, and place. Her work focuses on the complexities of breaking, healing, and holding steadfast when walls weaken and ghosts linger. IG: *@ajwojtalik.poetry*

Amanda Roth (she/her) is a poet whose work explores motherhood, embodiment, and the climate crisis. She is the author of the full-length collection, A Mother's Hunger (2021) and is featured/forthcoming in Rappahannock Review, Marathon Literary Review, MAYDAY, Moist, Blood Moon Poetry Press, and elsewhere. Web: *http://msha.ke/amandarothpoetry*

Amy Zender (she/her) is a good witch and old soul living duplicitously between Gemini and Einselkind. Oft saying: My Heart is Holding Your Heart's Hand, she disarms through words and meets folks right where they are. She has been married for 27 heartfelt years to a beautiful pilot, has two inspiring teens and two pups.

Angela Marshall (she/her) lives with her husband and daughters in the North East of England. She is an author, actress and playwright, and the author of her debut poetry collection, Not Just a Statistic (2021). She writes about miscarriage, greif and loss as well as her mental heath and trauma. IG: *@angela_writes_life_and_loss*

Anne Walsh Donnelly (she/her) is a single mother and lives in the west of Ireland. She writes poetry, prose and plays. Themes in her writing include sexuality, family, motherhood and mental health. Her poetry collection, Odd as F*ck, was published by Fly on the Wall poetry press in 2021. IG: *@Annewalshdonnellypoetry*

Cait Thomson (she/they) is a queer mama from Canada. She writes about her experiences with anxiety, trauma, parenting, and her love of nature. Her first chapbook is called we need another word for this love, (Bottlecap Press, 2022.) IG: *@cait.t.poetry*

Caitlan Docherty (she/her) lives in Illinois. She has a prairie view from her 4th floor apartment. Her work can be found in VAINE Magazine, blood moon POETRY, Sunday Mornings at the River, and Free Verse Revolution. IG: *@cmnpoetry*

Catherine Hamilton (she/her) lives in South London. She has been writing poetry since she was a teenager, but recently began to write more as a way of coping with a global pandemic and the pressures of parenting. Since then, she has had her poetry published in various zines and anthologies. IG: *@cathamcreates*

Céline de Moor is a Dutch writer who writes about the struggles and beauty of life. Her work touches on mental health subjects such as her compulsive disorder, eating disorder, depression, anxiety, and the pressure of society. Another passion of Céline is photography. IG: *@photographs_by_celine*

Courtney LeBlanc is the author of the full length collections Exquisite Bloody, Beating Heart (Riot in Your Throat) and Beautiful & Full of Monsters (Vegetarian Alcoholic Press). She is a winner of the Jack McCarthy book prize and her next collection of poetry will be published by Write Bloody in spring 2023. She is the founder and editor-in-chief of Riot in Your Throat, an independent poetry press. Blog: *wordperv.com* | IG: *@wordperv79*

Dallas Miller / d. h. miller (she/her) has lived in 2 countries, 6 states, 24 houses, yet only feels at home in a good red lipstick. Currently she is living in Florida, working from home while raising 2 feral children, chasing 2 domesticated canines, and sharing life's complexities with her husband of 28 years. IG: *@d.h.miller_penned*

Daniel Reyes (he/him) is from Seaside, California. He is a stereotypical Pisces, and feels blessed to be a part of this collection because writing is the healthiest way for his to conquer his demons. IG: *@xanielreyes*

David Estringel is a Xicanx writer with words at The Opiate, Red Fez, and The Blue Nib. He has had three books published, Indelible Fingerprints (2019), Blood Honey (2022), Cold Comfort Home (2022) with little punctures coming sometime in 2022, as well as three poetry chapbooks, Punctures, PeripherieS, and Eating Pears on the Rooftop. IG: *@david_estringel* | Web: *davidestringel.com*

Eddie Brophy is a poet, author, and blogger from Massachusetts. His previous writing credits include poems in Better Than Starbucks, Ghost City Press, and Terror House Magazine. His debut novel "Nothing to Get Nostalgic About," is available now on Amazon and wherever you get your books. His first poetry collection "Autumn's Eulogy," is available on Amazon from Book Leaf Publishing. IG: *@eddiebrophywriter*

Elaine T Stockdale is an Australian poet whose work covers a range of themes but has a strong focus on love, heartbreak and mental health. She has released two books, Love and Let Go (2020) and Paper Hearts (2021). Her poetry has also been featured in anthologies by Train River Publishing, Sunday Mornings at the River and Quillkeepers Press. IG: *@e.tstockdale*

Emily Ericson (she/her) is an illustrator from Texas with a B.F.A in illustration from Savannah College of Art and Design. She loves to create whimsical and engaging work for folks of all ages. When not creating, you can find her haunting local antique stores, exploring spooky old houses, or just reading a good book. IG: *@emilyeillustration*

Emiiy Perina (aka ESP) is a New York artist. Her crafts range from mixed media sculpture, to poetry, to welding, and most recently, taxidermy. She centers her work around attempting to accept her anxieties while pushing herself to adapt new practices to portray these feelings in her work. IG: *@esp_sculpture* | Web: *emilyperina.com*

Emily Perkovich is from the Chicago-land area and the Editor in Chief of Querencia Press. Her work strives to erase the stigma surrounding trauma victims and their responses. She is published with Sunday Mornings at the River, Cathexis Northwest, Coffin Bell Journal, and Awakened Voices among others. She is the author of the poetry collection Godshots Wanted: Apply Within and the novella Swallow. IG: *@undermeyou*

Emma Morgan is a poet based in Oxford, UK, whose work is woven with themes of motherhood, nature and self-reflection. Emma writes poetry when she cannot sleep, or while walking dogs. She has been featured by Bent Key Publishing and Small Leaf Press. IG: *@emmorpoetry*

Emerson Craig (he/him) is a first-year PhD student in Spanish Literature at the University of Iowa. He writes poetry on his experiences as a queer trans man from a tiny town in New England. He has two self-published poetry collections— I Cannot Hold these Birds for Long and Ghost of a Boy. IG: *@ghostofaboy_*

Gabrielle Vaigneur Wheatley (they/them) is a Kansas-based poet and short story author. You can read their work in Gypsophila Magazine, Pile Press, Chasing Shadows Magazine, as well as a myriad of other fine publications. When Gabrielle is not writing, they can be found playing Animal Crossing, walking in nature, making jewelry and other art, or playing with their dog, Lady Bird.
IG: *@gabriellevaigneurwheatley*

George Fisher (He/Him) is a poet/writer, originally from the UK, now based in Sydney, Australia. He has had several poems and articles accepted to both digital and printed publications, including the first Beyond The Veil anthology, There Is A Monster That I Am Learning To Love. IG: *@g.fisher.poetry*

George J Cardy (she/her) is from London, UK. Her poetry has been published in Sunday Morning at the River 2020 Winter Anthology, Crooked Jukebox: the 6ress, issue 2 and Issue 3 of the Latte Edit. She also has poetry featured in Free Verse Revolution Lit 'Issue 2: hermes, the kaleidoscope,' Mental Zines 'Issue 3: Inside,' the 1st issue of Handwritten & co Magazine and online publication Fizz. George has worked in theatre and television. IG: *@george.verses*

Hanna Webster is a San Diego-based science writer, poet, and graduate student in the Johns Hopkins University Science Writing Program. She has a B.S. in neuroscience and creative writing from Western Washington University. As a queer writer, she strives to highlight divergent ways of viewing the world that inspire beauty and critical analysis. You can read her work in Jeopardy Magazine's 55th issue, The Xylom, The Science Writer, and elsewhere. IG: *@ivory.daydream* | Twitter: *@queencortisol*

Heather C. Moll (she/they) lives on Treaty 7 territory, on the edge of the windswept Canadian plains. She is a deep-hearted queer poet and photographer. She's also a mom to two teenagers, nature-lover, autodidact, and work-in-progress. She's been published in Beyond The Veil's first anthology, Sweet Tree Review, and coming soon with Quillkeeper's Press. IG: *@heathercrystalk* | Twitter: *@heathercrystalk*

Jai-Michelle is Scottish born poet, living via London in The Netherlands. Originally an editorial journalist, she evolved into a singer songwriter, recording artist and performer. As a poet she is inspired by mytho-poetic inner landscapes, surrealism, and healing through complex PTSD through the unconscious. Her work has been published in several magazines including Free Verse Revolution Literary Magazine, The Mythos Poetry Society Journal and Calliope's Eyelash. Her first chapbook will be published by Sunday Mornings At The River (2022.) IG: *@bornonadarkmoon*

jeganmones (she/her) is a minimal line artist who creates everything with her index finger on her laptop's trackpad. She likes that her lines aren't perfect but, are still seen as a work of art. IG: *@jegan__mones*

Joe Rolnicki graduated from Moraine Valley Community College and Dominican University before attaining a Masters of Science in Education from Northern Illinois University. Joe grew up in the midwest and currently resides in Austin, Texas. In 2022, Joe published his first poetry collection, Second Adolescence, and hosts "The Other Poetry Podcast" on Spotify. IG: *@theotherjoerolnicki*

Joan Smith Green is a widow, mom, Jamma, sister, friend, and retired educator. She has survived rape; defeated alcoholism; earned a black belt in Kempo Karate; become disabled while working; loved and lost. She is learning to enjoy life and face its challenges. She is nurturing herself and healing by combining her deliberately cultivated positive outlook with words and art. IG: *@joan.s.green*

K. M. Crane (she/her) was born and raised in the southern-most corner of Northern California. Some of her work has appeared in Star*82 Review and IO Lit. She was a nominee for 2019 Best Microfictions, for which she is grateful. She serves as a Poetry Editor for Variant Literature. IG: *@k.m.crane*

Kate MacAlister is an author, feminist activist and founder of the community arts and literature project for womxn "Voices of Rebellion". Her works have been published in journals and anthologies all over the world. Her poems are stories of human connection and the dreams of revolution. IG: *@kissed.by_fire*

Katerina Bacher is a published poet from the Bay. Backed by her mixed heritage, extensive performance background, and a Bachelor's in sociology, her work focuses on identity, family, and the simple heartbreaks of being human. These days, you can find her either reading, singing, or daydreaming about what the world could be. IG: *@kbacherinawrites*

Katie Ness (She/Her) is a published poet with Hecate Magazine's: BIRTH and DECAY Anthologies, Poetry Undressed, Mulberry Literary, and others. Her poetry chapbook Aphrodite Fever Dream is published with Undressed Society Press. She is a yoga teacher living in London and an ectopic pregnancy survivor. IG: *@katie_wild_yogi*

Kris Kaila (she/her) is a Vancouver, BC poet, writer, book reviewer, and blogger. Her poetry and creative nonfiction has been published in an online magazine Harness Magazine. Kris is a Collab Fellow with The Poetry Lab and finds her passion in all things creative. IG: *@krisesque_life*

L.A. Roquemore (she/her) is a writer, a conversationalist, a professional photographer, an asker of ALL the questions, a practitioner of presence, a collector of moments, and an encourager of souls. She leads workshops for growing writers in Lakeland, Florida, where she lives with her three kids (and a cat!) IG: *@loveisanaction*

Lee Hodgins / Spellwriter (he/him) draws his inspiration from the human experience of working, living, and traveling the world, and from his experience in the fields of crisis support and human services. The content of his poetry isn't for the faint of heart and is meant as a meditation on some of our deepest fears, longings & taboos. He splits his time between the Canadian cities of Edmonton, Alberta and Victoria, British Columbia. IG: @spellwriterpoetry |
Web: *https://linktr.ee/Spellwrite*

Lucas Pearce is an Australian Poet, who grew up in Sydney and started writing poetry when he was sixteen. When he isn't writing, he's probably eating, on a bush walk, or celebrating the Chicago Bulls impending return to the playoffs. IG: *@lucas.pearce*

Lynne Ellis (she/they) writes in pen. Her words appear in Poetry Northwest, the Missouri Review, Sugar House Review, The Shore, and elsewhere. Lynne was awarded this year's Perkoff Prize in Poetry & the 2018 Red Wheelbarrow poetry prize. Their chapbook, In these failing times I can forget (Papeachu Press) considers the human cost of rapid growth in a prosperous American city. IG: *@stagehandpoet*

Madison Gill (she/her) is a female poet living, working, and building a tiny home in Colorado. She received her bachelor's degree in English from Colorado State University-Pueblo. Her work has appeared in print and online with publications such as Pocket Lint, Sledgehammer Lit, Tiny Spoon, Anti-Heroin Chic, and From Whispers to Roars among others. She is the 2021 Cantor Prize winner (Telluride Arts Institute.) IG: *@sweetmint_poet*

Marc Brimble (He / him) veganism Noun. the practice of not eating or using any animal products, such as meat, fish, eggs, cheese, or leather.
IG: *@marc.brimble* | Web: *marcbrimble.substack.com*

Melia Donk (she/her) is a writer, poet, artist and mental health advocate, based in Victoria, Australia. She works as a University Student Administrator, supporting students through their studies. She lives in a cute little regional town with a very fluffy tuxedo cat. IG: *@meliadonk*

Michael Roe lives in Arvada, Colorado. With a background in illustration, graphic arts, and digital art, he works in oil, acrylic, and pastel in an impressionistic style. His work is an award winner in the 2018 "This is Colorado" Show and was accepted to the Pastel Society of Colorado's "Small Works" Pastel Show. His memberships include the Art Students League of Denver and the Pastel Society of Colorado.
Web: *http://mdroe16.wixsite.com/mroeart*

Myheart_poetry (she/they) writes real-time poetry directly from the heart. She is a spiritual warrior who has completely redefined her life & identity in recent years. Her lenses include toxic relationships, sexual assault, compulsive heteronormativity, religious trauma, conversion therapy, coming out, divorce, sex negativity/sex positivity, queer relationships, break-ups, and motherhood. IG: *@myheart_pooetry*

Naomi Head (she/her) is a writer based in Edinburgh, Scotland. She is a confessional poet who uses poetry to process emotions and understand her place in the world. Naomi's work has been published by celestite poetry, Coin Operated Press, Beyond the Veil Press, little living room, Sunday Mornings at the River and many more. Web: *naomihead.com* | IG: *@naomieah*

Olivia Zhang (she/her) is a student and artist based in the United States. Always inspired by the world around her, she loves to experiment with textures, patterns, and contrast in her digital pieces. Olivia spends time making jewelry, reading poetry, and studying to piano music.

Rachel Dickens (she/her) is a mother, poet, writer, illustrator and designer based in Bristol, UK. She has been published by The Mum Poem Press, Mothership Writers, The6press, Positive Well-being zine, Motherzing, Gypsophlia, Freeverse revolution lit and more. IG: *@racheldickenspoetry*

Rainlily (she/her) is a poet who finds beauty even in life's sad moments. Writing is her way of releasing things that are too heavy to carry and rocessing life's more difficult seasons. She hopes that by being honest about her emotions and struggles, others might feel more connected and remember that they are not alone. IG: @ *rainlily_writes*

Rebecca Rijsdijk (she/her) (pronounced *Ricedyke*) is a poet and a carer based in Eindhoven, The Netherlands. Rebecca published 'You were married when I met you' (2020) as a way to process an emotionally abusive relationship. Followed by 'The Care Home,' (2021) and her fifth book, 'The Boy from Salamanca.' Rebecca also runs an indie poetry press called Sunday Mornings at the River. IG: *@rebeccarijsdijk* | Web: *rebeccarijsdijk.com*

Robin Cressman (she/her) is an artist and writer based in Southern California. She and her work are animated by the healing powers of nature, creativity, and love. Most days you can find her with sand between her toes, dirt under her fingernails, or the taste of salt water in her mouth. She lives with her husband, dog, and a lot of plants. IG & Twitter: *@robincressman*

Samuel Boerma is a Dutch writer based in Utrecht, The Netherlands. Since obtaining an MA in creative writing from Swansea University he's been working both as a writer and a journalist. His work previously appeared in Writer's Block magazine and Expanded Field journal, and is set to appear in Sunday Mornings at the River. IG: *@samboerma*

Sarah Eckstine (she/her) is a photographer and writer from Western Maryland who received her BFA in Photography from the Maryland Institute College of Art in 2020. She is currently pursuing her MFA at Illinois State University. Sarah's work focuses on her life as a woman with chronic health issues and borderline personality disorder. IG: *@saraheckstine*

Sidrah (she/her) is a 28 year old Pakistani Muslim poet based in the UK. She is a collector of hobbies and she dabbles in: photography, art, various martial arts, and of course, reading and writing. IG: *@writing.by.SA*

Simon Hauwaerts (he/him) is a young writer who was born and raised in Belgium. He studies English Literature at the University of Sussex. Simon will read and write anything, but his preferred genres are horror, poetry, and nonfiction. IG: @ *simonhauwaerts*

Sophia Mihailidis (she/her) is a 20-something year old living in Australia. She uses writing as a source of healing for her nightmares, both literal and figurative. When she isn't untangling her brain, she is completing her Masters of Education and working towards changing the education game for the future. IG: *@soph.eeah*

Sophia Murray (she/her) is a poet, witch, and NFT creator living in the wilderness of Northumbria, UK with a merry gang of wild animals (small human and canine in origin.) When she isn't writing she can be found doing laundry. IG: *@sim_poetry* | Twitter: *@sophiaisamurray*

Susan Niemi (she/her) is a Lesbian, Mom, and published poet. A survivor of incest, rape, and domestic violence, she writes openly about her trauma in an attempt to release the remaining pain, evict shame, and continue to nurture self-love. Her first published poem appears in There's A Monster Inside That I'm Learning to Love (Beyond The Veil Press.) IG: *@slniemi59* |
FB: */susan.niemi.165*

Stephanie Farrell-Moore is a Scottish actor, voiceover artist, writer and producer- hosting open mic events with @themumpoempress. Her poetry reflects all aspects of womanhood and she has a particular interest in the menstrual cycle and its influence on identity and creativity. Her inner seasons period poetry collection, Bleed Between The Lines, will be published later this year by Blood moon POETRY press. IG: *@stephfarrellmoore*

Troy Turner (he/they) lives in the Pacific Northwest where nature and society meet. When not serving the caffeine-deprived, he writes fiction and poetry. Currently his focus is on world building for a fantasy series. IG: *@troynturner*

Wynnie (She/her) is a poet and artist originating from the PNW. She now lives in the woods of southern Indiana, where she spends her free time hiking, drawing pet portraits, and writing. Her poetry reflects her personal struggles with anxiety/chronic illness. She also writes about love and the profound effect it can have on our lives and in the lives of others. IG: *@_bashful.violet*

Zoe Simmons (she/her) is an award-winning Australian journalist, copywriter and author who's been published hundreds of times around the globe—including by News.com.au, New York Post, Daily Mail, POPSUGAR, New Idea, That's Life and more. Zoe writes candidly about her experiences with bipolar, anxiety, and chronic pain and fatigue, in hopes of advocating for change, and helping others to feel less alone. IG: *@SomethingBeginningWithZ*

ABOUT BEYOND THE VEIL PRESS

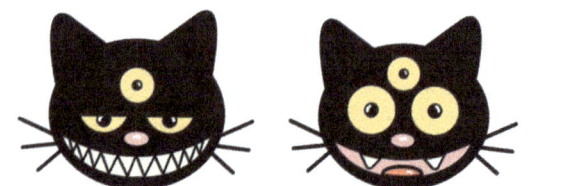

Beyond The Veil Press is an indie publisher of poetry & art, based in Colorado, and founded by two art school graduates in Spring 2021. We are strong advocates of Mental Health Awareness and donate a percentage of each book sale to a featured mental health nonprofit. True to our name, we love all things spooky, blurring boundaries, and shedding light on the mysterious unknown.

Whether you need support or hope to support a loved one, we encourage you to visit the Mental Health Resources page on our website.

Beyond The Veil Press is run by poet/artist/survivor **Sarah Herrin** (she/they), with the support of poet **AJ Wojtalik** (she/her).

Web: *beyondtheveilpress.com*
IG: *@beyondtheveilpress*
FB: */beyondtheveilpress*

MENTAL HEALTH RESOURCES

BOOKS

The Body Keeps The Score – Bessel van der Kolk
The Journey From Abandonment To Healing – Susan Anderson
Waking The Tiger - Peter Levine
Polysecure: Attachment, Trauma, & Consensual Nonmonogamy – Jessica Fern

WEBSITES

Active Minds - Mental health awareness and education for students.
activeminds.org

American Foundation for Suicide Prevention - Saving lives and bringing hope to those affected by suicide. *afsp.org*

Anxiety & Depression Society of America - Prevention, treatment, and cure of anxiety, depression, OCD, PTSD, and co-occurring disorders through education, practice, and research. *adaa.org*

The Trevor Project - Crisis intervention and suicide prevention services to lesbian, gay, bisexual, transgender, queer, and questioning youth. *thetrevorproject.org*

National Institute of Mental Health - Research on mental disorders. *nimh.nih.gov*

PODCASTS

Being Well - Rick Hanson, Forrest Hanson
Where Is My Mind? – Niall Breslin
The Savvy Psychologist: Quick & Dirty Tips – Jade Wu
The Hilarious World of Depression – John Moe
The Happiness Lab – Dr. Laurie Santos

APPS

Headspace: Meditation and Sleep Made Simple

More resources available on our website.

www.ingramcontent.com/pod-product-compliance
Lightning Source LLC
Chambersburg PA
CBHW080622200526
45165CB00036B/2088